THUNDERS SPEAK

Biographies of
Nine Special Original People

James Patrick Dowd

*with a
Contribution
by*
Dr. James A. Clifton

HERITAGE BOOKS
2012

HERITAGE BOOKS
AN IMPRINT OF HERITAGE BOOKS, INC.

Books, CDs, and more—Worldwide

For our listing of thousands of titles see our website at
www.HeritageBooks.com

Published 2012 by
HERITAGE BOOKS, INC.
Publishing Division
100 Railroad Ave. #104
Westminster, Maryland 21157

Copyright © 1999 James P. Dowd

"Captain Billy Caldwell: On the Reconstruction of an Abused Identity" by Dr. James A. Clifton, 1976
Used by permission.

All rights reserved. No part of this book may be reproduced or transmitted in any form or by any means, electronic or mechanical, including photocopying, recording or by any information storage and retrieval system without written permission from the author, except for the inclusion of brief quotations in a review.

International Standard Book Numbers
Paperbound: 978-0-7884-1135-9
Clothbound: 978-0-7884-9431-4

ACKNOWLEDGEMENTS

Throughout the years, I have had the privilege of corresponding, conversing and making friends with some of the most exciting and wonderful people in all this world. There are any number of Original People (or Native Americans as is presently the popular vernacular), who I count as friends, and who, I hope, include me as one who cares and loves them in the same manner. Again, there are other friends who I have had the pleasure of knowing in one way or another over the years who are not Original People in the sense that their ancestors where not among those who have claim to being descendants of the people who first inhabited the continents of North and South America. Twenty some odd years as an antiquarian bookseller has brought many close and abiding associations. Researching for some twenty two years has brought a flurry of grand acquaintances who regularly correspond, and yet, there are those, librarians, research associates, curators, amateur historians, authors, would-be authors and historical society directors and members who are the unknown heros behind any writers published works. My thanks to these - all my friends and incidental co-authors.

In the early 1970's, I made the acquaintance of one very special person; this was the man who was responsible for my start as a writer. Glen Adams, the Prairie Printer who owns and operates Ye Galleon Press in Fairfield, Washington wrote me a letter in 1973 and asked whether I thought that I might write an introduction for a reprint of J. B. Patterson's, "Life of Black Hawk." I agonized over this for some time, but finally managed to begin the necessary research, and some months later Glen had his introduction. The reprint appeared in a limited edition of 500 copies in 1974, and quickly sold out. Glen had created a monster! A full length book, "Built Like a Bear...," appeared in 1979 and "Custer Lives!," appeared in 1982. In 1988, "The Potawatomi a Native American Legacy," appeared. And in between I took up the avocation of being a freelance writer.

Along the way, I happened to begin a correspondence with James A. Clifton (who has kindly allowed use of his work on Captain Billy Caldwell.). Jim was a Frankenthal Professor of Anthropology and Ethnohistory who has had published numerous books and articles on our Original Peoples. His home base for many years was the University of Wisconsin at Green Bay. He has concentrated on the Potawatomi people, but has also written numerous essays on other indigenous groups as well. Jim was, in a sense, my mentor, much as he has been the mentor for numerous students who have had the pleasure of being instructed by him over the years. Whenever I became discouraged, it was Jim Clifton who always managed to send a letter which lifted my spirit and gave me the incentive to continue to learn and to continue to write. Jim is presently scholar in residence at Western Michigan University in Kalamazoo. My special thanks to my very special friend.

CONTENTS

LIST OF ILLUSTRATIONS vii
INTRODUCTION ix

CHAPTER 1 All Same...All Same... 1

CHAPTER 2 Big Foot Lake Man 17

CHAPTER 3 Captain Billy Caldwell: On the Reconstruction of an Abused Identity
by Dr. James A. Clifton 25

CHAPTER 4 For He Was A Bad Son 72

CHAPTER 5 Ghost Dance Woman 97

CHAPTER 6 The Idaho Giant 104

CHAPTER 7 Last of the Yosemites 117

CHAPTER 8 Prophet of Disaster 131

CHAPTER 9 Meet the First Light...and Die 146

EPILOGUE 161
SELECTED BIBLIOGRAPHY 163
INDEX 173

ILLUSTRATIONS

Shabni (He Has Pawed Through)	4
Pkuknoquah (Bear Clan Woman)	5
Brave Bear	73
Maria Lebrado—The Last Survivor	129
White Cloud—*The Prophet* by Catlin	136
Wabansi (The First Light) in 1836	150

INTRODUCTION

The Native Americans whose biographies form the content of this book all lived either in the center, or at the fringes, of a great thunderstorm. Among these ancient peoples of the Woodlands, the Plains, the Mountains, and the Great Desert, there was a spiritual belief which may have prevailed in various forms from time immemorial. A Potawatomi leader of the 1840's related this mystical rite to Father Pierre Jean De Smet in a lengthy dialogue which was later published in the noted Jesuit's famous book, "Western Missions and Missionaries." This following brief excerpt will be sufficient to introduce the theme of this book:

"The thunder we hear is the voice of spirits, having the form of large birds placed in the clouds. When they cry very loud we burn tobacco in our cabins to make them a smoke-offering and appease them ..."

This brief quote from a lengthy cosmology relation was given to De Smet by a man called "Potogojees,"(AKA Padegozhuk - Pile of Lead). And it tells us much more than the spiritual reactions of his people in a time of natural crisis. Without perhaps realizing it, Padegozhuk had, in a certain inexplicable manner, told us all that had befallen his people and all that would follow them into the present day. The allegory is this -The thunder can be equated with the coming of Euro-American civilization to the New World. The burning of tobacco symbolizes the initial friendship which the Indian peoples first displayed towards the whites, and the rising smoke can symbolize the gunsmoke which soon enveloped the continent. Thus, this great storm, with its driving rains and flashing lightning, was the impact of a clash of cultures. In the traditions of Original People, the Thunder is the voice of the Great Spirit; the burning or offering of tobacco is a gift to the great-grandmother and the rising smoke is the prayer of a people for unity and truth among all the peoples of this earth.

In the southern part of the North American continent, the Spanish created the first storms in a brutal fashion. Carib, Aztec, Inca, and Maya cultures were the first to be enslaved and destroyed. Indians of the Pueblos of the great desert soon felt the impact of the murky clouds, while the Indians of Florida and the southeast soon were covered by the deluge. In 1608 the French arrived and founded the city of Quebec. Soon

Courier des bois, voyageurs, and missionaries began to intermarry, trade and prositilize among the various Indian nations which they encountered. The French did not outwardly attempt to enslave or destroy Native American cultures in such a sanguine method as had the Spanish. Instead, they created a dependency among the native peoples. European goods - steel knives, tomahawks, beads, traps, cooking pots, utensils, blankets and sundry ornaments now inundated various Indian cultures. Whereas the Spanish unwittingly gave the Indian peoples the horse, the French gave them an unquenchable taste for European technology. At the same time great numbers of Frenchmen developed cultural ties among various Native American societies, and soon, some of these adventuresome Frenchmen became more Indian than European. These people eventually became assimilated into the native cultures. New France became a strange semblance of old France.

The French left an indelible imprint on the native cultures they encountered. Coming, as they did, from a European monarchial system, they soon created "chiefs," from amongst the Native American leaders. Christian religion and thought were fully adapted by some Indians, while others selected only portions of the new theology and assimilated it into their lives. Still other Native Americans clung tenaciously to the old ways.

The introduction of firearms created societal upheavals across the continent. Those tribes or nations who first came into possession of these new weapons began to push their more western and southern neighbors into great migrations. Abenaki and Huron fought their battles against the Iroquois. The Iroquois fought against the tribal groups which were south and west of them. The area around the Great Lakes was in process of transformation. Tribes such as the Erie and Illiniwek were nearly exterminated. The colonial expansion continued westward into the Dakotas where the Lakota/Dakota people had been displaced. The French had created a chain of events which was to change the face of the New World in North America, while Spanish influence would continue in Central and South America even until the present day.

During the 17th century other migrations from Europe to America were taking place. English, Dutch and Swedish colonies appeared along the eastern coast of North America. The people who came to these colonies were, for the most part, fleeing from poverty and religious persecution in the Old World. When the English arrived in America and came in contact with the Indian peoples they sought only to destroy them. An argument raged for some 200 years as to the humanness or lack of same of the Indians. The reasoning presented (as a pretext for annihilation) was as follows: Either the Indians were the Lost Tribe of Israel, or else they were nothing but animals, or beasts of the forests. This was the rationale for torture, persecution, confiscation of lands and eventual extermination. The Abbe Mac Geoghegan of the Irish Brigade in France, after the fall of King James, once remarked rather aptly, "A nation that wishes to enslave others, generally treats those who will not submit to its laws as savages..."The similarity between what had occurred in Ireland and America was striking.

Upon the ascendancy of the English over the French after Queen Anne's War, French forts in the west came under English occupation and colonists slowly spread across the Alleghenies. Native Americans slowly adapted to new trading partners. Indian peoples who lived west of the Great lakes area or on the Plains were beginning to be seriously inconvenienced by this turn of events, as pressures from Eastern Nations who had superior weapons, threatened their ancestral homes. It is true, the English were more sparing with trade goods, but generally the prices were somewhat more reasonable, and the quality of a better type. Many Native Americans never forgot their French friends, but the English soon gained a general acceptance. The Indians really had no choice.

The Revolutionary War and its aftermath changed everything for Native Americans. Here, indeed, was the eye of the storm. Once the colonists had won their independence from Great Britain, a massive influx of adventurers, land speculators, whiskey peddlers, ne'er-do-wells and honest settlers inundated the Ohio Valley. This trespass on to Indian lands culminated in a series of bloody military battles in the 1790's. The Treaty of Greenville in 1795 brought an uneasy calm to the frontiers. For all intents and purposes this treaty and the Louisiana Purchase a few years later marked the beginning of the end for Native Americans. The Treaty of Ghent in 1815 which ended the War of 1812 between the Colonies and Great Britain signalled a massive era of treaty making - treaty making intended to move the now decimated and demoralized Indian populations from the most desirable lands. This treaty making was a strange potpourri - One country purchased the land from another country for cash in hand, and then proceeded to repurchase the land from the original inhabitants. These white men were certainly strange creatures!

The treaty making initiated by the United States in 1778 continued unabated until the facade was dropped in 1883. Then, in 1887, The Dawes Allotment Act threatened the last vestiges of Native American communal society. Again, in the 1950's and 1960's, ill-advised politicians attempted a policy of "Termination" on Indian reservations. The lure of money to an impoverished people caused a very few of the reserves to become abandoned to the detriment of the native societies. These people were cut adrift in the runoff of the great storm waters of a culture that offered them no alternatives to the old ways. They were to become assimilated into a society which still remained foreign to the ways of peoples whose existence centered around a spirituality and oneness with the earth, the creatures of this earth, and all that was a part of the universe as they conceived it. It proved to be a disaster for those unfortunate enough to be caught up in the maelstrom. Through it all, the various original peoples have survived with many of the values of their respective cultures still somewhat intact. Acculturation and assimilation had not occurred. Adaptation and confrontation have formed the leaking shelters into which the native peoples have sought refuge.

The various monographs herein presented hopefully will offer the reader an unusual cross-section of voices from the past. These are the ancestors; both (in relative terms), good and bad. You will meet travelers, warriors, shamans and leaders. You will see the faces of many, in photographs, paintings and sketches. You can look into the eyes of some of these people, and perhaps, read the determination, spirit and pathos in some of those piercing windows of the soul.

A few words of caution are needed as the reader embarks on this journey into the midst of the thunders. Certain words will not be used, except where direct quotation (s) make it necessary. Some of these inflammatory words or "catch-alls" are squaw, papoose, half-breed, red men or copper skinned. Instead, they are replaced with (squaw), woman or lady; (papoose), child, baby or infant; (half-breed), Metis; and (red men or copper skinned), with Original People, Indian, or a direct tribal designation. I continue to use the designations "whites," or "white man," whenever other more proper ethnic names are unavailable. Terminologies such as Euro,

Afro, Anglo, or Asian American seem to me to be too restrictive although, at the present time, they are the more acceptable forms in generalized usage. Placing people into ethnic groupings is many times a necessity, but I often think how wonderful it would be if such allusions could someday disappear.

And perhaps someday, the great thunderstorm which surrounds our Original Peoples, and other minorities throughout this shrinking blue planet of ours will also disappear, but I have no illusions...

JAMES DOWD

1999

CHAPTER 1

ALL SAME . . . . ALL SAME . . . .

They called him barbarian,
Uncivilized man.
He sounded forth no clarion,
His name he could not write.

They called him "Friend of White Men,"
Castrated brother.
He sold their land with X of pen,
He bargained for a nation.

A grove of timber was given him,
For all time.
It was taken at a whim,
He blacked his face and left.

On his way he met a friend,
Civilized man.
And here all rime must end.
He said, "White Man called him,
Damned Indian."

With tear stained eyes,
He looked heavenward and said,
"No damn Indian, no damn White Man,
All Same . . . . All Same . . . ."

This was God's barbarian.

©1989, Jim Dowd

OTTAWA/FRENCH - (POLITICAL POTAWATOMI)

SHABNI - pronounced as Shahb-knee, (HE HAS PAWED THROUGH, or, HE PERSEVERES FOR LIFE) Ca 1783-1859. Variant spellings for the name are as follows: Chabona, Shabonna, Shabbonah, Shaubena, Shabenee, Shabeny, Shaubeanee, Shabenai, Shabenay, Shabehney, Shambly, Chevalier, Chamblee, Chambli, Chambly and at least another twenty variations. Shabni had the distinction of being known in Illinois by two different titles - "The Paul Revere of Illinois," and "Friend of the White Man." This first title or sobriquet was earned at the beginning of the so-called Black Hawk War. The second title was given him by the Sac and Fox after the Black Hawk War. He was a man whose life was a paradox in many ways. He tried to live in two worlds, transcending Indian and White cultures, but in the end, he died, a man, broken in spirit. He should have been accorded the renown reserved for those who have led a full and good life, instead, during his final days, he became merely an object of curiosity. His story deserves to be told and he deserves, even at this late date, a measure of respect, some mark of honor, as one of the greatest of all the Native Americans who ever graced this continent. Hear then, the tale of a warrior, and a real human being. He was truly "Aneshnabeg," the Ottawa word which designates, "Original or Real People."

Shabni was born of Ottawa/French parentage probably in Michigan. The date of his birth, as is the case with most birth dates for early Native Americans, is in doubt. No records were kept, and the date was furnished by Juilette Kinzie who interviewed Shabni in 1833. Shabni told Mrs. Kinzie that he was about twelve years of age in 1795 when his father took him to meet General Anthony Wayne at Greenville, Ohio. We also know that his parents were living at Cross Village during the early 1800's, as his nephew Andrew J. Blackbird of Arbre Croche, Michigan (Original person name),Mackatebenessy, which actually means Black Hawk) mentioned in his book, "History of the Ottawa and Chippewa Indians of Michigan." Blackbird's mother was sister to Shabni's mother, and another nephew was William (Petanakwet), who studied for the Roman Catholic priesthood in Rome, but was assassinated just prior to his ordination.[1] Cousin to all was Augustin Hamlin Jr., (1813-1862) a broker and self proclaimed "chief" of the Ottawa of northern Michigan who was part French, Chippewa and

Ottawa.[2] This is all we know for certain of Shabni's ancestors.

One early document which places Shabni in the historical record is a relation of Dr. John Cooper, surgeon of Fort Dearborn (Chicago). The document is drawn from a verbal account of Dr. Cooper presented to a man named James Grant Wilson. This brief mention of Shabni occurred prior to 1811, probably about the years 1807-8, (no actual date is given).

"The most prominent Indian with whom Surgeon Cooper came in contact while in the West was Shabbona for whom he successfully prescribed without charge, when the young chief was suffering from some sickness. I saw Shabbona in Illinois before his death in 1859. He was of tall and massive figure, was pleased to hear of the pale face medicine man who had cured him of his illness at Fort Dearborn some five decades earlier ..." [3]

Shabni's first biographer was a pseudo-historian and romantic, named Nehemiah Matson of Princeton, Illinois. Matson claimed that Shabni had told him that he (Shabni) had first met the famous Shawnee leader, Tecumseh in 1806; that Tecumseh rode into his village in De Kalb county, Illinois astride a coal black horse, and, from that time forward he became a true believer in the message that Tecumseh related, viz., that a coalition of all the Indian peoples and a return to the old ways would stop the relentless advance of the Chemokemans (Great Knives, as the Americans were called).[4] Around he year 1810, Shabni married into a Potawatomi band. The first wife's name has not been handed down to us, but we know that she bore at least two children to Shabni. Pkuknoquah, (Bear Clan Woman), was Shabni's primary wife and faithful partner throughout his long life. She was the daughter of a Potawatomi leader named Topnibi (He Sits Quietly), a man who claimed the distinction of being "chief of all the Potawatomi." He later married a number of other women as was the custom; one other Potawatomi wife was named Zebequah (River Woman), another Nebebaquah, (Night Walking Woman), of Kickapoo origin, and also possibly the French/Potawatomi woman named Victoria Pothier in 1833. There is secondary information that he had possibly yet another wife, whose name is unknown as yet, and who may have been of Cherokee origin.

Shabni (He Has Pawed Through) Ambrotype taken in 1857.
Courtesy: The Chicago Historical Society   ICHi-08746

Pkuknoquah (Bear Clan Woman) Ambrotype taken in 1857.
Courtesy: The Chicago Historical Society   ICHi-08742

If Shabni was born about the year 1783, it is not unreasonable to assume that he may have fought in various battles in which the Ottawa, Chippewa and Potawatomi were engaged in during the period 1800 onward. In 1800, Shabni would have been about seventeen years of age, an age when most Indian youth experienced their first trials on the path of war. Although his name is never mentioned in any records of this time, it is highly probable that he was a respected warrior at an early age. Why else would Tecumseh of the Shawnees court this man in 1806 to eventually become his aide during the War of 1812?

On November 7, 1811 was fought the terrible battle of Tippecanoe just north of present day Lafayette, Indiana. This battle was a prelude to the western phase of the War of 1812. Governor William Henry Harrison with a force of approximately one thousand men met an Indian force of approximately the same size. The Indian allies who comprised the Indian army were members of numerous tribes such as the Shawnee, Potawatomi, Ottawa, Kickapoo, Delaware, Wea, Sac and Fox. The great leaders on the Indian side were Stone Eater, Winnemac, White Loon, and a man named Shobbonier (French-Chevallier).5 This latter French/Odawa leader has, for all the intervening years from 1811 to the present been confused with Shabni. Shabni did not fight in the Battle of Tippecanoe, and always denied having done so.

We know for certain that Shabni fought in the War of 1812 with the Indian allies on the British side. On the 15th of August, 1812, under orders from General Hull at Detroit, Captain Heald commander of Fort Dearborn (Chicago), evacuated that fort and headed south along the western shores of Lake Michigan. A force of four or five hundred Potawatomi warriors attacked the unfortunate column which consisted of fifty-four privates, two officers, twelve militiamen and about a dozen women and twenty children. At the termination of the battle, some fifteen Indians had either died or been wounded, and there remained only twenty five noncommissioned officers and privates and eleven woman and children left alive from Captain Heald's force. Shabni was not present at this battle, or massacre, but arrived on the scene shortly thereafter. He had numerous friends at Fort Dearborn, notably the American Fur Company trader, John Kinzie and his family. Shabni, ever the man of empathy for his friends went to the Kinzie cabin, along with a man named Chandonnai at the termination of the battle and was effective in helping to save the lives of the Kinzies and others.6 The story of the Fort Dearborn "massacre" became the subject of bar room tales over the years, and most accounts today are filled with the vivid imagery of those long ago tavern dwellers.

During the War of 1812, Shabni had the distinction of being a Captain in the British Indian Service.7 He acted as second-in-command to Tecumseh and was present at the two battles of Fort Meigs, Maguaga, Fort Stephenson and Frenchtown. At Frenchtown, a glimpse of the humanity of Shabni became evident.8 After this battle, a number of wounded prisoners were confined in a deserted cabin. They were guarded by two British soldiers. Among these men was a young man named George Shelby, a nephew of Governor Shelby of Kentucky, and a lieutenant in a Kentucky regiment. During the night, a party of Indians overpowered the guards, rushed into the cabin and began to slaughter the prisoners. Into this slaughterhouse came Shabni. He immediately rushed in among the murderers and began to throw one this way, and another that, and caused them to desist from their bloody work.9 Shabni visited the young George Shelby for many days afterward while he was detained in hospital. Many years later, in 1835, when Shabni was in Washington, D.C., Shelby greeted him and gave him a fine gold topped cane and top hat.

The fortunes of the British and Indian allies in the Old Northwest were quickly fading. After a disastrous affair at Fort Stephenson, near Sandusky, Ohio, the allies under the British general Proctor, made a hasty retreat to Canada. Upon being shamed by Tecumseh as being "unfit to wear a woman's petticoat," Proctor, at length decided to take a stand at the Thames river at Moraviantown. This was to be Tecumseh's last battle. There are any number of claimants who related the death of Tecumseh. However, Shabni's account as first related in the "Chicago Democrat' in 1840 would seem to bear the truth. Shabni related how, as the Kentucky mounted volunteers charged the Indian lines, Colonel R.M. Johnson (later Vice-President of the United States under Martin Van Buren), shot Tecumseh at point blank range as that warrior raised his tomahawk to strike Johnson. Tecumseh died instantly. Shabni then led the retreat of his Indian forces, and it would seem that they were in a desperate position. Shabni mentioned that, at the time, he prayed to the Great Spirit, that if they (the Indian force) were allowed to escape, he would never again raise the tomahawk against the White Men.[10] The Great Spirit answered Shabni's prayers, and after the battle Shabni and a number of Shawnee warriors recovered the body of Tecumseh. For Shabni, the war was over. He returned to the Illinois country and the age old life of trapping, hunting and the making of sugar in the cool groves. His longtime friend and associate, Captain Billy Caldwell gave a relation concerning himself and Shabni in 1840. Caldwell had become interested in the Presidential campaign of William Henry Harrison, and wrote from the Council Bluffs Reservation, the following:

"To General Harrison's Friends:

The other day several newspapers were brought to us; and peeping over them, to our astonishment we found that the hero of the late war was called a coward. This would have surprised the tall braves, Tecumseh of the Shawnees and Round Head and Walk-in-the-Water of the Wyandotts. If the departed could rise again, they would say to the white man that General Harrison was the terror of the late tomahawkers. The first time we got acquainted with General Harrison, it was at the council fire of the late Old Tempest,'General Wayne,' on the headquarters of the Wabash, at Greenville, 1796. From that time until 1811, we had many friendly smokes with him; but from 1812 we changed our tobacco smoke into powder smoke. Then we found General Harrison was a brave warrior and humane to his prisoners, as reported to us by two of Tecumseh's young men who were taken in the fleet with Captain Barclay on the 10th of September, 1813, and on the Thames, where he routed both the red men and the British, and where he showed his courage and his humanity to his prisoners, both white and red. See report of Adam Brown and family, taken on the morning of the battle, October 5, 1813. We are the only two surviving of that day in this country. We hope the good white men will protect the name of General Harrison. We remain your friends forever.

Chamblee (Shawbonee) Aid to Tecumseh

B. Caldwell (Sauganash) Captain Tecumseh"[11]

Shabni is not heard from after the Battle of the Thames again until 1816. He was then in St. Louis where he signed his first treaty as a political leader for The Illinois River Potawatomi with the United States commissioners Ninian Edwards, William Clark, of Lewis and Clark fame, and Auguste Chouteau.[12] It was rumored at the time that words passed between Clark and Shabni.

In Gurdon Saltonstall Hubbard's book, "The Autobiography of...PA-PA-MA-TA-BE 'The Swift Walker,'" Hubbard mentions meeting Shabni for the first time at the American Fur Company station on the Illinois river in Bureau county in 1818. Hubbard was clearly impressed with Shabni, as he related the following: "...Shaub-e-nee was then about twenty-five years of age, and was, I thought, the finest looking man I had ever seen. He was fully six feet in height, finely proportioned, and with a countenance expressive of intelligence, firmness and kindness..." Hubbard continued, "I cannot close this communication without adding my testimony regarding the character and services of that noble Indian Chief, Shaub-e-nee, From my first acquaintance with him, which began in the fall of 1818, to his death, I was impressed with the nobleness of his character. Physically, he was as fine a specimen of a man as I ever saw: tall, well proportioned, strong and active, with a face expressing great strength of mind and goodness of heart. Had he been favored with the advantages of education, he might have commanded a high position among the men of his day. He was remarkable for his integrity, of a generous and forgiving nature, always hospitable, and until his return from the West, a strictly temperate man, not only himself abstaining from all intoxicating liquors, but influencing his people to do the same. He was ever a friend to the white settlers, and should be held by them and their descendants in grateful remembrance. He had an uncommon retentive memory, and a perfect knowledge of the Western country. He would readily draw on the sand or bed of ashes, quiet a correct map of the whole district from the lakes, west to the Missouri River, giving general courses of rivers, designating towns, and places of notoriety, even though he had never seen them." The two remained fast friends throughout their long lives, although Hubbard shared all the prejudices of his day. In Shabni's declining years, Hubbard told how Shabni stopped to visit with him in Chicago. This was a customary surprise visit from Shabni and members of his family. Hubbard had "important" guests in his fashionable home at the time, and afforded Shabni his woodshed as an accommodation.

From 1816 through 1833, Shabni was signatory, as a political leader, to all the important treaties which the Illinois River Potawatomi negotiated with the United States. Present day Potawatomi generally feel that the land cessions made by their people in days gone by were very unfavorable to them, however, if one looks at the records of treaty payments and other sundry transactions, it soon becomes apparent that Shabni and his fellow negotiators were quite good at their trade. The Potawatomi of Illinois (actually the United Nations of Potawatomi, and very small contingents of Ottawa and Chippewa, and known today as the Prairie Band), received more dollars per acre than any other tribal groups ever received throughout the entire history of treaties. But, no matter what the Indian peoples received in currencies, it could never offset the losses of their homelands, the graves of their ancestors or the terrible years of removal and attempted forced acculturation which resulted.

In 1827, a series of events occurred in southwestern Wisconsin and northwestern Illinois. Distraught at the forcible abduction and "hard usage" of some Winnebago women on the Mississippi river by boatmen from Fort Snelling, indignant Winnebago warriors rose up and committed "outrages" in the aforementioned areas. The Glazier family was murdered at Prairie du Chien, Wisconsin and a number of boatmen from the original marauding party were killed. Tensions ran high, especially at the newly rebuilt Fort Dearborn. The Winnebago had solicited aid from the Potawatomi, and a number of the Potawatomi Wkamek (leaders) still rankling over offenses committed against them were ready to join in a frontier war of attrition. During the 1827 annuity payment among the Potawatomi at the fledgling city of Chicago, a well known Potawatomi from southeastern Wisconsin acted in a very suspicious manner. This man was called Big Foot (Makesit). He was supposedly very angry. He was thought to be belligerent. The resident population of Fort Dearborn reacted to him in panic, and called forth their known friends, Shabni, Billy Caldwell, Alexander Robinson (sometimes known as Chechebinway (The Squint Eye,) and Shemargar (Soldier) to act as spies and attempt to ascertain the disposition of Big Foot. The four heroes of this adventure rode off to Big Foot's village some fifty miles north of Chicago. Now, Billy Caldwell would be in serious difficulty at the village, since he was not Potawatomi. He was half Mohawk and half Irish. Alexander Robinson would also have difficulty as he was of Scottish-Ottawa blood and Shemargar was little known among the Wisconsin people, as he was a Potawatomi leader from the Kankakee river area of Illinois. So, instead of entering the village, Billy, Alexander and Shemargar used discretion and allowed Shabni to enter alone, while they looked on from a distance. The stories of Shabni's harrowing experiences at the Big Foot village (or the Winnebago village) vary at this point; some say he was taken captive by Big Foot and threatened with death, some say he simply entered the village and talked with Big Foot as to his intentions, and others maintain that he used a stratagem to secure his freedom. Further, it was said that he only stopped at Big Foot's village and his captivity occurred among the Winnebagos as he traveled farther north into Wisconsin. Whatever occurred, Shabni managed to calm Big Foot and/or the Winnebago and make a safe return to his village. In a matter of days the whole scare ended when word arrived at Fort Dearborn that Red Bird and Wesaw of the Winnebagos were taken captive by Thomas L McKenney at gun point..., actually cannon point. The two were placed in confinement and Red Bird pined away and died within one year, while We-saw lived and was pardoned by President John Quincy Adams in 1828. As an aside to all this "Winnebago scare of 1827," this writer finds himself fortunate to have met, admired, and called friend a great-great-great grand nephew of Red Bird (Mitchell Crowe) who lives, works and dreams the dreams of old - yet lives and works in the White man's world to make a good life for his family. Shabni had nothing to do with the Winnebago per se, but he did manage to persuade the more militant Potawatomi leaders not to support the cause, thus assuring that the Bodewadmi (The Keepers of the Fire) would remain as a people, and not suffer total annihilation. The Potawatomi would not become ready victims of a Holocaust.

In the fateful year of 1832, Shabni was to shine forth as a savior to the settlers of Illinois. This was the year when a terrible conflict called the Black Hawk War began. This was the year when a stain upon the verdant prairies and groves of Illinois commenced. Shabni was supposedly called into council at Tiskilwa, Illinois (then called Indiantown), with the Sac (Osagiwuk-People of the Inlet). The leader of the so called British Band, Makataimeshekiakiak (The Black Sparrow Hawk) acted as guiding spirit in the council. The Sac leader feted Shabni and other Potawatomi leaders and according to tradition, the following conversations occurred in council: Black Hawk and Wabokishiek (White Cloud) mentioned to Shabni that if the Sac and Potawatomi united their warriors they would be like the trees in a forest. To which Shabni replied, "The soldiers of the Chemokemans will be like the leaves on those trees."12

Black Hawk had lost his village just above Rock Island, Illinois through various intrigues. The land west of the Rock river in Illinois was then known as The Military Bounty Land.[13] The land had been awarded to veterans of the War of 1812 as public lands at their disposal. Black Hawk, perhaps misunderstanding British advice to his lieutenant, Napope (The Soup or Broth), and the admonitions of Wabokishiek (White Cloud), also known as the Winnebago Prophet, decided that he and his band had the force of law at their disposal. With a mounted force of some eight hundred warriors and families, they crossed the Mississippi river at Oquawka, Illinois with the intention of forcing a legal issue. They arrived at the Prophet's village at the present site of Prophetstown (aptly named) on the Rock river and headed north through Dixon, Illinois. At this point in time there had occurred no depredations or warlike encounters. Upon arriving at a place now called Stillman's Run in northwestern Illinois, a drunken rabble which purported to be an army commanded by Major Isaiah Stillman caught up with the rear guard of the Sac. The first and terrible encounter occurred in a densely wooded area at twilight. In Black Hawk's Autobiography,[14] he related how he, with only forty warriors watched the advance of Stillman's two hundred plus troops. Wishing to avoid a conflict, Black Hawk sent forth emissaries, who were promptly either shot or taken prisoner.

    Outnumbered as he was, the Black Sparrow Hawk decided to attack in what he thought was a suicidal mission. Almost instantly lead balls began to whistle through the air as the dreaded war whoop rent through the pristine forests. At least twelve of Stillman's men were killed outright, and a total panic enveloped the remainder of the befuddled army. Forty Indian warriors were soon pursuing a mob. Illinois volunteers never knew a more disgraceful day.

    In the meantime, Shabni, with his son Peckwani (Smoke) and a nephew set out on a mission of mercy which should never be forgotten by the people of the state of Illinois. Starting at Princeton, Illinois about 130 miles west of Chicago, Shabni began to scour the prairie and give warning to the settlers. Some one hundred disgruntled Potawatomi had also taken advantage of the turmoil, and old grievances were foremost on their minds. At risk of live and limb, Shabni virtually flew across the prairies on his pony. "Boszho, nikan, ahaw puckagee" (Hello, friend. now, you must leave!) became a password which numerous pioneers did not always fully understand. When this was the case, Shabni reverted to the very basic rudiments of the English language that he knew, and with gesticulations he made himself known. Entering La Salle county at a place called Indian Creek, he warned three families; the Halls, Davis and Pettigrew's. The male members of these families were generally "Indian Haters." On one occasion William Davis beat Shabni's son-in-law Mehoki (translation unknown) for complaining about Davis' damming of Indian Creek. On May 21, 1832 some twenty (some say forty or sixty) Indians attacked the tiny settlement and killed fifteen of the settlers. The Hall daughters, Rachel and Sylvia Hall were taken captive. James Davis, a lad of seven years of age was also taken captive, but when he couldn't keep up with the war party he was unmercifully shot through the head. When an armed party of citizens from Ottawa, Illinois arrived at the scene, the carnage was described as gruesome. The female victims were suspended from the door frames upside down; their private parts cut away, while the children were seen with heads smashed asunder against trees. Eventually the Hall girls were ransomed by the Winnebago after being subjected to indescribable terrors among the Sac.[15] Shabni had warned not only the Indian Creek settlers, but a host of others. Upon reaching the settlement of Millbrook on Fox river, Shabni's pony dropped dead from exhaustion. A grateful settler named Hollenback gratefully gave Shabni a second horse. Shabni continued eastward towards Chicago, warning all as he went. Hollenback barely escaped from his claim with his life. Had Shabni arrived even an hour later, he and his family would have been massacred. Hollenback and his family ever after remembered the name of Shabni in fond remembrance. Upon the termination of the Black Hawk War, Shabni was henceforth called, "Friend of the Whites." Shabni acted as a war leader in a scout battalion during the so called Black Hawk War and he was accompanied by almost all the then important leaders of the Potawatomi nation. The important leaders of his adopted nation agreed with him unanimously. In 1905, a monument was raised at Indian Creek. A modest sized monolith recognizes the Indian Creek victims, while nearby, a second spire stands by the victims' grave. This shaft is dedicated to Shabni!

    Once peace came to the frontiers of Illinois, Shabni returned to live at his village of over twenty years, and which had earlier been reserved to him and his Illinois River Potawatomi band, via the Treaty of Prairie du Chien in 1829. This village was located in De Kalb county, Illinois "near the Pawpaw Grove." The reservation consisted of two sections of land (1,280 acres), well watered and well timbered lying on both sides of Indian creek, and originally called "Shabnee's Grove.". It was located near a natural ridge of high land and distant enough from most white settlements to afford Shabni and his band a haven. In 1836, the first removal of the Illinois Potawatomi, according to the terms of the Treaty of Chicago of 1833 began in earnest. Shabnee's Grove was a gathering place along the route of removal and Captain J.B.F. Russell requested Shabni to assist in leading the Illinois Potawatomi westward. He soon returned to the Illinois reservation in 1837 and for a brief period of time, he and his family lived in harmony with the first settlers. Soon, however, an onrush of settlement began. These newcomers had come from the eastern United States for the most part, and were generally uncaring as to any "Indian" having any rights whatsoever. Throughout the 1840's, the Shabni band rented out small portions of the reservation. This was done in order to obtain an income while the family traveled back and forth to Council Bluffs, or simply when they went on extended visits to friends. Shabni and his band had fenced and otherwise made improvements to the land, especially so, the area near his lodge and Shabni burial ground.

 Some of these new settlers who had come to Illinois were the outcasts of eastern society and before long "the banditti of the prairie" began to steal, murder, and commit outrages throughout the area. Through a series of frauds, bribes, and mis - representations to the United States government, Shabni's reservation became the object of an assault by these nefarious people. Finally, in 1849, while Shabni was absent on an extended visit to his tribe who were now living in Jackson County, Kansas on the Prairie Band Potawatomi reservation, to collect his annuities, his reservation in Illinois was declared abandoned by the General Land Office and illegally sold at public land auction. Upon returning to his reservation in De Kalb county, Illinois he was cursed at, whipped, and driven off his reservation. Now in advanced years, he blacked his face in sorrow, and with his family retinue of twenty plus, he headed eastward. It was at a place called "The Big Woods" that he met a pioneer friend, Tracy Austin. The poem which prefaces this monograph gives the simple, yet eloquent, comments by Shabni: "All Same...All Same..."

In 1857, Shabni's grand and faithful friend Perry A. Armstrong, an attorney of Morris, Illinois, with the aid of numerous citizens of the state purchased a plot of twenty acres for the aged leader and his family. The land was along the south edge of the Illinois river on high ground. Armstrong was adroit enough to have the land taken off the La Salle county tax rolls so that it could never be taken from Shabni or his family. It remains that way even today.[16]

In 1859, Shabni took a chill after returning from a hunt, and died at his home on the 17th of July. Prior to his death, Shabni had commented that he wanted no monument for his grave. In all the simplicity of his heart, he remarked, "The life I live should be my only monument."

Shabni fought for the return of his reservation which had been solemnly recognized by the formal Treaty of 1829 until his death in 1859. After his death, his wife, Pkuknoquah, continued to live in Illinois with her daughters and grand children. The sons had returned to the Kansas Prairie Band Potawatomi reservation.[17]

Pkuknoquah continued to live at Morris, Illinois until her death in November of 1864. She died, under mysterious circumstances, after falling from a "Democrat" wagon into Mazon creek. To add to the tragedy, her four year old grand daughter Mary was trapped beneath her body and was suffocated. Following her death in November, 1864, the remainder of the family removed to Kansas to rejin their people and become a part of the reservation experience. Husband, wife and a number of family members are buried in Evergreen cemetery at Morris, Illinois. In 1903, a memorial boulder was placed on the gravesite.

The story of the man who "Pawed Through," and his heroic wife as related by this author is brief. It is perhaps, after all, only a monograph in a thunderstorm.

NOTES

1. Blackbird, A.J. History of the Ottawa and Chippewa Indians of Michigan; A Grammar of Their Language, and Personal and Family History of the Author. Ypsilanti, Mich.,1887.
2. Clifton, James A. On Being and Becoming Indian Biographical Studies of North American Frontiers. Chicago, Illinois, (1989).
3. Chicago Historical Society Collections.
4. Matson, Nehemiah. Memories of Shaubena. Princeton, Illinois,1876. & Matson, N. Raconter/Four Romantic Stories..., Chicago, 1882.
5. McCollough, Alameda (ed.). The Battle of Tippecanoe: Conflict of Cultures. Tippecanoe County Historical Association, Lafayette, Indiana 1973.
6. Dowd, James P. Built Like a Bear...Shabni (He Has Pawed Through). Ye Galleon Press, Fairfield, Wash., 1979.
7. British Colonial Papers - London, England.
8. Patterson, J.B. (Amanuensis). LIfe of Black Hawk... Boston, 1834.
9. Ibid note #6
10. Ibid note #6
11. Kappler, Charles. Indian Affairs, Laws and Treaties. Vol. II, Interland Publ. Co., New York, (1973). See preamble, page 132.
12. Ibid note #8
13. Ibid note #8
14. Ibid note #8
15. Records LaSalle County Court May 21, 1834.
16. Whitney, Ellen (ed.). The Black Hawk War. Vols. XXXV, XXXVI and XXXVII, Illinois Historical Collections. 1970, 73, 75.
17. War Department Records. Reserve File A-416.

CHAPTER 2

BIG FOOT LAKE MAN

Big Foot (Makesit) is a virtual unknown among early Native American leaders. He left no known legacy. He just simply seems to have disappeared in time. Like others of his era, he suffered at the onrush of European civilization. Because his skin was dark, he was forced to leave the beautiful lake where he and his people had lived for years.

What little that is known of this man's life is now recorded. There are no grand deeds or heroics; only perhaps the telling of a tale of one whose life happened to coincide with the era which his people might have called "The Time of Tears." Thus, with no excuses or apologies - THE LIFE OF BIG FOOT LAKE MAN...

POTAWATOMI

Big Foot Lake Man - That's only this writers appellation for Makesit. Makesit means simply Big Foot, and whether the name was a clan name, a warrior name or a nickname is unknown. If the name was a clan name, my best guess is that it was an eagle clan name. A few pseudo-historians have claimed that he was named after the shape of the lake upon whose shores he lived, but this is really quite improbable. It does not fit into the manner in which Great Lakes peoples were named. The year of Big Foot's birth is unknown; probably sometime in the late 1780's or '90's. He is described (in an unflattering manner) first by Mrs. John H. (Juliette) Kinzie in her book, "Wau-bun/the 'Early Day' in the North-West."[1] Mrs. Kinzie's narrative and remembrances of Big Foot are not dated in her book, but from "Lockwoods Narrative,"[2] it would appear that her sketch was drawn from a meeting with him in 1823-4.

"Soon, after mid-day, we descended a long, sloping knoll, and by a sudden turn came full in view of the beautiful sheet of water denominated Gros-pied by the French, *Maunck-suck* by the natives, and by ourselves Big-foot, from the chief, whose village overlooked its waters. Bold, swelling hills jutted forward into the clear blue expanse, or retreated slightly to afford a green, level nook, as a resting place for the foot of man. On the nearer shore stretched a bright gravelly beach, through which coursed here and there a pure, sparkling rivulet to join the larger sheet of water.

On a rising ground, at the foot of one of the bold bluffs in the middle distance, a collection of neat wigwams formed, with their surrounding gardens, no unpleasant feature in the picture. A shout of delight burst involuntarily from the whole party, as this charming landscape met our view.

It was like the Hudson, only less bold - no, it was like the lake of the Chapel of William Tell! What could be imagined more enchanting! Oh! If our friends at the east could but enjoy it with us! We paused long to admire, and then spurred on, skirting the head of the lake, and were soon ascending the broad platform, on which stood the village of Maunck-suck, or Big-foot.

The inhabitants, who had witnessed our approach from a distance, were all assembled in front of their wigwams to greet us, if friends-if otherwise, whatever the occasion should demand. It was the first time such a spectacle had ever presented itself to their wondering eyes. Their salutations were not less cordial than we expected. 'Shaw-nee-aw-kee'* and his mother, who was known throughout the tribe by the touching appellation 'Our friend's wife,' were welcomed most kindly, and an animated conversation commenced, which I could understand only so far as it was conveyed by gestures-so I amused myself by taking a minute survey of all that met my view.

The chief was a large, raw-boned, ugly Indian, with a countenance bloated by intemperance, and with a sinister, unpleasant expression. He had a gay-colored handkerchief upon his head, and was otherwise attired in his best, in compliment to the strangers."

Mrs. Kinzie goes on to relate much on the scenery, and only comments once on the hospitality that Big Foot and his people offered to her and her party. In a sense, I suppose, her recollections of Big Foot might have been distorted somewhat over the years as her book was first published some thirty-one years after the events she so deftly penned, and Big Foot, as will soon be seen was thought of by the inhabitants of early Chicago as an evil Indian, not to be trusted.

All of this "trouble" with Big Foot started, or at least came to the fore in 1827. Big Foot and a deputation from his village had come to Chicago to share in their annuity payments. As the story goes, a fire broke out in the rebuilt Fort Dearborn, and Big Foot and his fellows refused to assist in putting out the blaze. This really shouldn't have been so surprising to the pioneers of early Chicago. After all, Big Foot and his people were not trained as volunteer firefighters! If a wickiup happened to catch on fire in a village, and there were no people trapped inside, these people would have simply let nature take its course. After all, what matter was it to build another habitation? Cut some cedar poles, stick them in the ground at preset intervals, cover the whole with bark or skins, leave a centrally located smoke hole, start a warm fire in the central hearth, and home was restored. No mortgage either! But, the American Fur Company agents, those who dealt in "Indian Floats," and nefarious Indian agents decided that Big Foot and his people were probably involved in an intrigue with their neighbors, the Winnebago, and might be planning an attack or uprising against the pioneer community in northern Illinois. Thus, friendly Indian and Metis agents were dispatched to the village on Big Foot lake to ascertain whether or not this Wkama (leader) was so disposed. The story as given in numerous chronicles afterward were so distorted that the actual occurrences today can hardly be called reliable.[3] Suffice to say, Big Foot and his people remained at peace and never threatened the fledgling pioneer community.

One thing which I have neglected to do, up to this point in my narrative, is mention something of the area where Big Foot's village existed in those early days. Today, the lake, upon whose shores he and his people lived is called Lake Geneva. It is located in the extreme southeast corner of the state of Wisconsin in Walworth county. It was named after a town in New York which, in turn, was named after the lake of the same name in Switzerland. Property along the shores now sells for a minimum of one thousand dollars per square foot of shore line, and it truly is a beautiful lake. The town of Lake Geneva stands upon the eastern edge of the lake, while the town of Williams Bay, where Big Foot's village was located stands at the northwest end of the lake. The beaches today are sandy, but the gravelly substrata of the lake is notable to the tender footed wader. The lake is of great depth-some say two-hundred feet at its deepest, but for that I cannot attest. In Big Foot's day, there was a trail which had its beginning at Chicago and its terminus at the town of Galena, Illinois.[4] This trail led directly through Lake Geneva on the way to Galena, Illinois (Greek word for lead) which was the center for the lead mines as far back as the late 1700's, and it was the Indian peoples themselves who first made use of this mineral ore.

Returning at this point from my digression on the territory and lake of Big Foot, I continue forward in time. Among a number of questions which should be asked about Big Foot, is whether or not he signed any treaties. Was he simply a village leader, or a true member of the grand nation of the Potawatomi? The answer is that he was truly a grand member/leader (wkama) of the Potawatomi. He was also a man who was to suffer terrible grief; grief so terrible that people of our day and age can only sympathize with this human being. First - the treaties..., Makesit signed the following treaties during his lifetime, with his name badly distorted by translators on almost all of them: The Treaty of Chicago-1821, as "Mauk-see," The Treaty at the Missionary Establishment on the St. Joseph river in Indiana-1828, as "Mank-see," The Treaty of Prairie du Chien, Wisconsin-1829, as "Maw-geh-set," The Treaty of Chicago-

1833, as "Mang-e-sett," The Treaty of Chicago (Supplementary)-1833, as "Mans-kai-suk," Treaty of Chicago (Supplementary)- September 27, 1833, as "Mang-e-sett," and finally The Treaty of Council Bluffs, Iowa-1846, as "Mah-suck."[5]

And now, it is time to speak of the sorrows which beset Big Foot. In 1836, he "lost a son whose body he had caused to be encased in a rude coffin and fastened to the limbs of an oak, some forty feet from the ground and overlooking the lake. He gave as a reason for this novel form of sepulture that his son was unusually fond of lake scenery and he wished him to enjoy a fine view of it from that country to which he had gone. The usual mode of burying among the tribe was by a slight burial in the earth, protecting the graves from the inroads of wild beasts by a small covered pen made of trees. They usually deposited with the dead, food, tobacco, trinkets and other articles of which the deceased was fond, or which they imagined he would use in the state to which he had gone."[6]

The brief narrative appended above is interesting in some respects, but the reality is that the author of years past was unaware of true Potawatomi burial customs. Generally, deceased individuals were placed in blankets and covered with bark, or, as in the above case placed in rude coffins in large trees. After the flesh had disintegrated the remains were taken down and placed in the ground where small grave houses were placed over the deceased. Various rituals were performed for specified periods of time at this site, with the thought in mind that the spirit of the departed would be pleased to leave this earth for a new and better world. Breaches in the ceremonial rites which attended interments could have serious repercussions to the living if the ghost or spirit of the deceased were to return.

Only a few years earlier, Big Foot's young wife also had died. Her name has not survived her, but there is, today a life size wood sculpture which represents and bears tribute to her on the shores of Lake Geneva on Williams Bay.

With the passing of these two members of his family, the time for the emigration of the Potawatomi people from their homeland to the short grass prairies of the west was ready to progress. A notice of Big Foot's final day at Lake Geneva was recorded by an early chronicler, a Reverend Durnnell, as follows: "Big Foot's band was all gathered into his village at the head of the lake, so as to be taken to Chicago. This was in the month of September. James Van Slyke had removed to that point a few weeks before, and his family were living in a partially finished log cabin, in full view of their encampment. Noticing one morning a great commotion in the Indian camp, and not knowing the cause of it, he imagined that an outbreak upon the white settlers who had trespassed upon their lands was contemplated. For some reason not now known-he fled for his life, leaving his family in the cabin. Mrs. Van Slyke watched every movement of the savages through the unchinked walls of her dwelling. After a time she was relieved of anxiety by seeing them pack their movable property upon their ponies and squaws, and taking a trail towards the South, disappear one after another through a wooded ravine.

After all were gone as she supposed, Big Foot appeared, and proceeding to the council-house and placing one arm around the signal-pole, stood for some time in silence, thoughtfully viewing the scenes which had been familiar to him from childhood and which he was never to behold again... After this silent leave-taking the chief walked over to see Mrs. Van Slyke. Leaning his tall form against the doorless doorway of the cabin, he talked kindly to the woman who was ever a friend to his race, and then, bidding her a final farewell, turned away to join his band, and was seen no more."[7]

According to the terms of he Treaty of Chicago of 1833, Makesit and his band headed towards the rendezvous point in the Big Woods along the DesPlaines river some twelve miles west of Chicago. On November 1, 1837, he accordingly enrolled himself and followers for removal and left for Shabnee's Grove some forty miles west. For some reason not recorded, the Big Foot party decided that they would not be removed by the government contractors. This was a wise move indeed, as the removal, as it turned out, was truly a trail of death for the Potawatomi. Instead, Big Foot, along with 842 men, women and children, voluntarily left for the western lands. They were unescorted, committed no depredations and settled that first winter and spring along the Skunk and DesMoines rivers in western Iowa. They finally left this area and settled with their people at Council Bluffs, Iowa on the United Bands reservation. Big Foot and his followers thus formed the core of six (perhaps seven) wkamek (leaders) who lead the Potawatomi, Ottawa and Chippewa peoples who had been forced from Michigan, Indiana, Illinois, andWisconsin during the initial removals.[9,10] The people who remained in Council Bluffs and later settled at Mayetta, Kansas became known as the Prairie Band.

It was said by at least one chronicler that Big Foot was still alive as late as 1867, but this is uncorroborated.[11] The last treaty he signed was the Treaty of 1846 at Council Bluffs. Had be been alive in 1867, it is quite possible that would not have signed the treaties of 1861 and 1867. Neither of these treaties were totally acceptable to all the Potawatomi, and in some cases, are not fully accepted even today by modern Potawatomi people. It's a shame that more is not known about Big Foot. That he tried mightily to hold on to his home on the shores of Lake Geneva, and thus may have been party or instigator of a plan to side with the disaffected Sac and Fox and Winnebago is probably true. But, when his own people spoke out against war, and called for cooler heads, Big Foot gave his promise to remain at peace. He was ever a man of his word. It would seem that the thunders caused a mighty flood of rain to fall on this man, and yet, as seen in the story of Mrs. Van Slyke, he offered no recrimination or vengeance. Big Foot is long since gone to the land of spirits. If he was Eagle clan, then surely this mans spirit has flown to a better place.

NOTES

1. Kinzie, Mrs. John H. Wau-Bun, The early Day in the North-West. New York, 1856.
2. Collections of the State Historical Society of Wisconsin, Madison, Vol. II, 1903. (reprint edition).
* "Shaw-nee-aw-kee." John Kinzie, called by the Potawatomi as Silver Man.
3. Collections of the Historical Society of Wisconsin, Madison, Vol. VI, 1908. (reprint edition) Hubbard, Gurdon S. Appended statement by..., in "Kingston's Recollections."
4. Collections of the State Historical Society of Wisconsin, Madison, Vol. XII, 1892. Thwaites, Reuben Gold (ed.). "The Story of the Black Hawk War."
5. Portrait and Biographical Record of Walworth and Jefferson County, Wisconsin. (Chicago, 1894).
6. Ibid note #5.
7. Ibid note #5.
8. National Archives, Record file M-574, Roll 14, #98. "Emigration of Potawatomi Indians."
9. Clifton, James A. The Prairie People/Continuity and Change in Potawatomi Indian Culture 1665-1965. The Regents Press of Kansas, Lawrence, (1977).
10. Edmunds, R. David. The Potawatomis/Keepers of the Fire. University of Oklahoma Press, Norman, (1978).
11. Ibid note #5.

CHAPTER 3

CAPTAIN BILLY CALDWELL: ON THE RECONSTRUCTION OF AN ABUSED IDENTITY

The following study of Captain Billy Caldwell is the work of the distinguished scholar Professor James A. Clifton. It is taken from an expanded version of a paper presented in a syposium on Ethnogenesis on the Great Lakes Fronties at the annual meetings of the American Historical Association 30 December 1976 in washington, D.C.[1]

James A, Clifton's research on Captain Billy Caldwell as represented in the following essay is a milestone. Billy Caldwell's life and accomplishments have been misrepresented for some one hundred fifty plus years. He is seen, for the first time as a real human being, rather then as a caricature of frontier bar room tales.

Enter the real Billy Caldwell...

MOHAWK-IRISH

In the decades after Pontiac's resistance movement the vast territory surrounding the Upper Great lakes was the setting for a series of extensive, rapid, and irrevocable social and cultural changes. As the influence of New France waned, leaving stranded numerous old-settler Francophones, the agents and representatives of the British Empire arrived to establish themselves and their interests in a social milieu already transformed by more than a century of culture contact. Far too swiftly to allow establishment of many steady-state institutions or stable polities, agents and citizens of the fledgling United States pressed in, soon diminishing, then dislocating British power, now leaving behind numerous Anglo-Saxons and Scots-Irish to adjust their nationalities, if not their basic values.

On the southern sidelines, briefly, a cancerous Spanish imperial aspiration was acted out, occasionally swaying events ever slightly. Eventually, from the northeast, the first wavelets of a distinctive Canadian nationality would lap on the shores of the American States being carved out of the Old Northwest Territory, affecting the ambitions of persons and the choices made by communities. In some of these communities lived small groups of African slaves, owned by members of the British and American elites, or an occasional Black captive taken and adopted by one of the societies indigenous to the area. Further complicating the the linguistic and cultural composition of the populations residing in the were immigrant fragments of tribal groups from the Eastern Woodlands and places north of Lakes Superior and Huron.

Around the Great lakes lived the-for a long while-numerically dominant remnants of the segmentary tribes and chiefdoms indigenous to the region.[2] By the last quarter of the eighteenth century none of these societies occupied the same estate had been controlled and exploited by their ancestors. None was organized socially according to ancient, precontact designs. None followed the same adaptive strategies as had warmed and rewarded their grandfathers. All were caught up in the vast, global processes John Bennett has called the ecological transition.[3] Each was increasingly influenced by far distant economic and political events. All had become technologically dependent on the products of remote factories; and each was a frequent supplier of raw materials and manpower for distant markets and conflicts. All were caught up in a web of asymmetrical alliances with more powerful nation states and more balanced ties with neighboring rival tribes; and all were experimenting with new strategies for coping with their transformed and rapidly changing social environments. Every one of these societies was adding new instrumental skills to old roles, testing variant forms of social relationships, trying out novel styles of leadership, experiencing fresh forms of community life, and incorporating a miscellany of culturally alien persons into their villages.

During unstable periods of history cultural borderlands such as the Great Lake region are settings for high rates of innovation in both cultural and social forms, as well as for abortive revitalization processes and powerful social movements. They are places where personal identities are conflicted and altered, as individuals migrate from one social milieu to another during their lifetimes, when they pioneer new roles-especially those of patron, client, middleman, or broker, and while they attempt to adjust their private sense of worth and propriety to the public demands of radically opposed membership and reference groups. Intercultural borderlands are, moreover, settings where-once the genuine excitements of the frontier have passed by-folklore and legendry take over to fix acceptable images of key historical figures, sometimes tarnishing memories of them, sometimes buffing them to an eye-dazzling shine, generally pressing the complexities and subtleties of a person into moulds fashioned by ex post facto stereotypes and late developed ethnic categories.

Obviously there are numerous avenues leading to improved understanding of what we call ethnogenesis-the development of new group identities, distinctively different cultural forms, and new reference groups in the Great lakes region.[4] My companions have elected two alternative paths, Helen Tanner that of an assessment of the nature of a culturally heterogeneous community, and Jacqueline Peterson an explication of an important type of social network.[5] So as to bring our analysis closer to the reality of human experiences, I have elected to present a life history sketch of one individual. This approach, I believe, will better reveal some of the complexities of the distinctive cultural and identity processes of the period, as well as underscoring the dangers of continuing use of conventional, contemporary racial categories and ethnic nomenclatures as if they were analytically valid scientific constructs.

Billy Caldwell-in the public identities that were ascribed to or assumed by him, as well as the sense of personal identity he developed for himself-is the subject of this inquiry. Captain Billy Caldwell, Indian Department-the official title he himself preferred throughout his adult years to the time of his death-is an apt choice for these purposes.6 His years, from about 1782 until 1841, span the period of our concern nicely. During his lifetime he lived in a wide variety of different frontier communities, from the refugee Mohawk village near Niagara where he was born, to the new trading administrative center at Council Bluffs, where he died. In these years he was also continuously entangled in a variety of membership groups, reference groups, and social networks-British, American, Metis, tribal, and intersocietal. Similarly, throughout his life he has ascribed to him or he assumed diverse public identities, which varied with the social situations in which he found himself. Successively, these included the roles of child in a Mohawk matriclan and family, bastard son in a composite Irish-French Canadian household, student in a Jesuit school, Indian trader, clerk in the Kinzie-Forsyth trading establishment, Captain in the British Indian Service, American appointed "medal" chief to the Potawatomi villages in northern Illinois, husband-in series-to some four short-lived wives, father of about ten-also short-lived children, and, eventually, the position of business agent-advocate for the Prairie Bands of Potawatomi, an innovative role which he himself helped to establish.

Anticipating later discussion, let me remark that it is clear Captain Billy was not born into a Potawatomi totem ("patrician"), while their is no evidence to suggest that he was ever properly adopted into one of these basic Potawtomi descent groups. Thereby, lacking membership in a totem and having and Anglo-Irish father, he could not have been awarded nor could he have acted out the role of a traditional, clan-based wkama ("leader").7 The role of Potawatomi "Chief" that he later played was one of Euro-American derivation: it involved the duties of an intercultural broker.8 In 1829, when Alexander Wolcott arranged to have him appointed during the negotiations at the treaty of Prairie du Chien, Caldwell was not the first but only the most recent in a long series of aliens denominated chiefs over the Potawatomi by foreign authorities.9 The first such appointment documented was that of one Wilmet ("Catfish"), a supporter and client of Robert LaSalle, the outside power who in 1681 elevated this immigrant Wabunaki to a place of importance among the Potawatomi.10

Similarly, the personal name the Potawatomi allegedly gave Captain Bill cannot be used as evidence either for tribal membership or chieftainship. Indeed, this phrase, <u>Sakonosh</u> ("The Anglo-Canadian"), was a Potawatomi label for one of the different categories of people they recognized as populating their universe. <u>Sakonosh</u>, thus, is a Potawatomi name for an ethnic group, not a personal name at all. The Potawatomi sometimes referred to this man as an Anglo-Canadian because that is how they perceived and classified him, and because that is how, throughout most of his life, he identified himself ethnically. When they wished to address or refer to him by a personal name, Potawatomi <u>wkamek</u> ("leaders"), regularly called him by the personal name given him by his step-mother, Suzanne Baby-Billy Caldwell.11

To get Caldwell's several public identities into focus we have to recognize him for what he was, the product of special, unstable conditions on an intercultural frontier. Like many others of his kind, Captain Billy's birth was the consequence of the convergence of several opposed cultural policies as well as various individual needs. From the perspective of the tribal societies involved, one fashion of arranging and solidifying economic and political alliances was to present the opposed parties with valuable favors, particularly women. In the Potawatomi's experience this mode of relating themselves to Europeans in northeastern Wisconsin in 1658, when they concluded difficult negotiations by sending Radisson and Groseillieurs "dames bearing guifts," following which, it is recorded, "there was much mirth," and, presumably, later offspring.12 In the tribal viewpoint women were one of the rewards and children the cement of a new alliance.

However, Billy Caldwell's gestation was the product of events far to the east of Potawatomi territory and of a second, convergent, cultural policy, one which eventually helped to subvert the aspirations of the tribes involved. There, by the time of his birth in 1782, this tangential policy was exemplified in the practices of Sir William Johnson, as well as lesser agents, traders, and entrepreneurs on the western New York and Pennsylvania frontiers.

Such men had long come to recognize that there was more to be had than transitory release and domestic comfort in passing relationships with tribal women. When properly socialized the children of such unions, they had seen, were valuable human resources who could be employed as clients and middlemen, extending the reach of their father's ambitions.

These were unsettled times, before fixed, European institutions had emerged on the frontier. For many years there was no single, agreed upon, customary way of categorizing, classifying, sorting, and treating those children who were produced by liaisons between isolated men and tribal women. Billy Caldwell, for example, was born just seven years after the new category "half-breed," had been named in English print. Throughout much of his life he lived in social settings where such terms enjoyed little currency, and where a person was not automatically and arbitrarily categorized on the basis of the cultural fictions of "blood" and "race."[13] Instead, he spent his young adulthood in circumstances where people were classified ethnically on the basis of cultural, linguistic, and behavioral attributes. He was, to be certain, subject to social discrimination; but not on the basis of his "race." In describing how he was wounded on the River Raisin in 1813, for example, Major John Richardson-Canada's own historian of the War of 1812-described him as "Mr. William Caldwell," a courageous gentleman from Amherstburg who was "attached to the Indians,"[14] Here Major Richardson displayed the formal snobbery of a regular British officer by denying Captain Billy the rank he held in the British Indian Service. Similarly, one may search fruitlessly in the extensive Canadian documentation, from, to, and about Billy Caldwell for any reference classifying him as "Indian," "half-breed," or the like.

Several methodological and interpretative issues are at stake here. Such words as "white," "Indian," "half-breed," and the like are elements in the cultural semantics of inter-and intragroup relations characteristic of particular societies during certain periods in their histories. Hence the study of the origination and diffusion of such social race categories can tell us much of the development of socio-economic class systems in the Great lakes area, about changing male-female and family relations, about the transformation of egalitarian into inegalitarian communities, about varying norms and opportunities for social mobility, and about the growth of Canadian-American ideologies of group relations, ideologies that differed between themselves, while being based in common on increasingly popular folk-biological explanations of human nature.[15]

To employ such categories as "half-breed" uncritically, as if they were valid scholarly ideas, is to allow oneself to be conceptually imprisoned by the stereotypes found in primary documents or those expressed by informants. Employing such folk stereotypes naively indicates, at worst, some implicit acceptance of American racial ideologies or, at best, the commission of two fundamental methodological errors. Anachronistic interpretation, the second deadly sin of historiography, is one of these. In this respect it is a mistake to interpret Billy Caldwell's character and behavior in terms of his supposed "half-Indian blood." Through most of his life the category of "half-breed" was not in general use, while in his later years when such thinking did achieve greater popularity such stereotypes were only occasionally and erratically applied to him. Ethnocentrism, a major delinquency for anthropologists, is the other source of interpretive error. I suppose we may conveniently put these together and speak of ethnocentric anachronisms-attributing the categories, motives, and values of a contemporary culture to one in the past.

It is in this sense that Billy Caldwell's identity has been abused. Treated as a stranger, he has been perceived as an example of a category. The defining attribute serving to categorize him so is the easily noted marker of "Indian blood." Thus categorized he has had imputed to him a stereotyped collection of motives, values, and other attributes. Accepting the stereotype, those who have written about him after his death have been sensitized to perceive evidence supporting how he exemplified the category of "half-breed," while ignoring much readily available information that requires a more complex portrayal. In particular, the special cultural matrices in which he acted out the several roles he assumed during his life have been slighted, while the views and assessments of significant others in his life have been selectively bypassed and the ideals he set and assessments he made of himself totally ignored. This commentary outlines, I believe, explicit directions for a reconstruction of Billy Caldwell's historic identity.[16]

In the 1960's not many Prairie Potawatomi could remember oral traditions concerning Billy Caldwell. As it turns out, this was because none of his many children survived him and, hence, there was no descent line to perpetuate his name, power, and memory. The very few Potawatomi who claimed recollections of the man could tell very little of him, except that he was an important person. No details of his life were forthcoming, aside from the specifics of his death. As a very old man-more than seventy, so I was told-he was severely injured during a buffalo hunt on the western prairies. While chasing after a great bull his pony stumbled and rolled on him, badly breaking his hip. Carried back to his <u>wigwam</u> on a horse-litter to recuperate, late that night he recovered consciousness and tried to mount his youngest wife. This unprescribed exertion ruptured a major artery causing him to bleed to death. Not recalling much about the man, my informants at least arranged for him an appropriate, masculine passage, vigorous to the last breath and embraced by dangerous youth. These elder Potawatomi males hinted broadly Billy had been done in, that he might have gone on for many years except his wife-with a younger lover on the side-wanted rid of him and had cooperated with unwarranted enthusiasm in his last act.

American and Canadian folk images of Billy Caldwell's life story are more numerous and somewhat less fantastic than this Potawatomi fragment. These tales agree on certain alleged facts and vary widely in others. They differ from the Potawatomi account mainly in selective exclusion, and by projecting different needs for alternative kinds of folk heroes and anti-heros. Although dignified by later printing, all are based either on late nineteenth century American and Canadian oral tradition, received and written down third and fourth hand, otherwise one upon the other. None give much attention to contemporary documents, particularly Captain Billy's own extensive correspondence, or to information about his life provided by his brothers and others significant to him, those who grew up with the man, who lived, worked, served, and fought by his side.[17]

These traditions agree that Billy's father was probably William Caldwell, an Irishman who was variously either a Captain or Colonel in the British army. About his mother there is some confusion. She is made to be a Potawatomi, or a Shawnee-indeed, Tecumseh's own sister, or a Wendat. Given a Potawatomi mother, Captain Billy's tribal affiliation is explained, since the Potawatomi were a "matrilineal race," a conclusion these profoundly patrilineal, patrilocal, and patridominant tribesmen surely would have disputed. Awarded a Shawnee mother, Tecumseh's sister, Caldwell's supposedly close relationship with that heroic figure is accounted for. The

Wendat maternity, in the end, is closest to the Iroquoian truth, but this tradition seems to reflect no more than the recognition by some that Father William had nothing to do with either the Potawatomi or the Shawnee at that critical time before his son's birth, while he and his family had been closely associated with the Wendat beginning in the Spring of 1782. Unfortunately, this latter relationship developed after the birth of Billy, who was William Caldwell, Sr.'s eldest son.

Billy's birth year, in these accounts, is guessed at about 1780. Educated by Jesuits at Detroit, he became fluent in English and French, as well as several "Indian dialects." After 1807 he was closely associated with Tecumseh, serving that leader as personal secretary. Billy Caldwell's service in the British cause during the War of 1812 is recognized but slighted, except for a few glorified episodes. Two of these establish a central theme in the larger, later assessment made of the man. In one, on 16 August 1812, he arrives at Fort Dearborn too late to prevent the massacre, but in time to spring from his canoe, to cry "I am a man...Sau-ga-nash," and to stay the bloody tomahawk then about to fall on the bowed heads of the Kinzie family.[18] In the other incident it is related how Billy tried to save the life of a wounded Kentuckian in January 1813 at the Raisin River fight, only to have a bowie knife thrust through his throat for his troubles. Clearly, in spite of all, Billy would become a good friend to the "whiteman," particularly Americans.

In these official biographies Billy remains in Canada a few years after the treaty of Ghent, but in 1820 he changes his allegiance and moves to Chicago. There, in 1826, he is appointed Justice of the Peace and Election Commissioner. Simultaneously and curiously, he is a Potawatomi chief, a position he has occupied since before the War of 1812. Once established in Chicago his promise of friendship to the "whiteman" is kept. He is, so the tales go, instrumental in keeping Mangesit ("Big Foot") at peace during the 1827 Winnebago scare, while in 1832 he labors to safeguard American lives and property during the Black Hawk debacle. As part of his reward the American government builds him a frame house, the first in Chicago, while later Mark Beaubien honors him by calling Chicago's first hostelry "The Sau-ga-nosh." Thereafter Billy Caldwell serves Americans nobly by persuading his nation, the Potawatomi, to bow to the inevitable, to sell their Illinois and Wisconsin lands, and to move westward. He reaches the peak of his popularity in 1833 at the Treaty of Chicago, which effectively ended Potawatomi control and occupation of lake Michigan lands. "Chief" Caldwell then moves his nation west beyond the Mississippi, where he dies in 1841.

In all of these accounts Billy Caldwell is categorized as a "half-breed," which-given American racial thinking automatically made him an "Indian." In all of them as well, save the most recent, he is judged to have been a lustrous figure on the frontier, a truly noble savage, and an excellent friend to Americans. His Potawatomi name, as noted, was <u>Sakonosh</u>, which is not Potawatomi personal name at all; or else-marking his very erect six feet, he was called "Straight Tree," which is straight out of James Fenimore Cooper, not the Potawatomi lexicon of personal names. Had these tribesmen remarked his height and posture, they would have done so by nicknaming him "Stumpy" or "Gnarled." Similarly, because Billy was a good Indian, even in his sex life, legend gives him but one wife and one child, both of whom, tragically, pre-decease him.

The most recent attempts to create a useful image of Captain Billy add little to an understanding of his character or life history. One such effort labels him an "Indian Politician and Entrepreneur," and expresses some surprise that an "Indian," even a man who was a "mixed-blood," might achieve such distinction. This essay, written in keeping with late twentieth century concerns with anti-heroics and ex post facto moralizing, tarnishes the man's image with a negative "nation."[19] The second such effort expresses a different opinion and is of an entirely different type. Early in the 1970's a small network of people living near Detroit organized themselves as a pressure group, claiming to be the legal descendents of the "Billy Caldwell Band of Potawatomi Indians," a group they claimed had occupied much of the Ontario Peninsula in the nineteenth century. This group had very specific, practical goals: they were pressing an old and greatly confused claim against the Canadian government for lands on the Lake Erie shoreline, including Point Pelee and Pelee Island. In the newspaper furor that accompanied their campaign, Billy Caldwell was promoted to a "great Potawatomi chief and a British army colonel" and was said to have been an Indian hero second only to Joseph Brant. This newest folk biography of Captain Billy selectively pieced together fragments from the life histories of at least four separate men, including Billy

Caldwell, his father, William Sr., Lieutenant Colonel, the Baronet, Sir John Caldwell, and an actual, if obscure, historical leader of a tiny Ojibwa community that did in fact occupy Point Pelee early in the nineteenth century. This imaginative reconstruction was apparently cast and polished to a high luster with the aim of bedazzling Canadian authorities.[20]

Contrasted with a larger series of documented facts which are undistorted by racial stereotypes all these folk portrayals of Captain Billy Caldwell's life and identity quickly lose their plausibility. For example, there can be no doubt that William Caldwell, Sr., was his father, and none that their relationship was highly conflicted. These facts the elder Caldwell acknowledged in his Last Will and Testament, dated January, 1818 and probated after his death in 1822.[21] In this document the father, after handing over his valuable estate to Billy's younger half-siblings, admitted his paternity in one phrase, while in the next line he skillfully disinherited Billy-his eldest son, effectively blocking any further claim on the line of inheritance to the old partisan leader's eight younger sons and daughters. In this fashion William Caldwell, Sr., abruptly terminated a painful relationship, one that had been marked by his own grave inattention, by a lack of nurturance, and by painful discord since the time of Billy's birth some thirty-six or thirty-eight years earlier.

Billy's birth date is attested to by himself. In 1834, writing from Chicago, he addressed himself to his younger half-brother with these words, "Dear Francis...you will recollect this day will mark the 52nd time that St. Patrick has gone over my head."[22] The date of the letter was March 17th. Thus Billy asserted that his birth occurred in 1782, while also claiming unto himself as personal saint that figure who was also patron of his father's homeland. Written more than a dozen years after he was deprived of his patrimony, there is no uncertainty about Billy's continuing, strong attachment to his family and to the vital memory of his father, nor much doubt that he was laying claim to an Anglo-Irish ethnic identity. These are curious sentiments for an adult man, one so badly handled by his immediate kin, and-particularly-one who in 1834 was supposedly a Potawatomi "chief." However, I believe it likely that Billy was being inventive about his birth date; possibly in an effort to dispel any ambiguities about his origins and who he was. In the biographical sketches they provided Lyman Draper years later, both William, Jr., and James Caldwell, for example, expressed the conviction that Billy had been born in 1781 or a year earlier, while neither noted the St. Patrick's Day birthdate, a fact that should have been worthy of remark.[23]

One interesting document supports this inference, that Billy was born in 1780 or before. Probably written by Daniel Claus and dated 1780, it consists of a "Mohawk Song and Dance," and it is addressed to "Little Master Caldwell." Transcribed in Claus's clumsy Mohawk, it is difficult to obtain a full and accurate translation of it two hundred years later.[24] What can be teased out of these four short lines of Iroquoian prose are the (approximate) phrases, "Greetings...to the small abandoned one...(who is) Good Tom." The rest are mainly Mohawk nonsense syllables, of the sort that accompany simple chants. This document, which Claus went to the trouble of having printed, seems to have been for some sort of celebration, perhaps a birthday. Daniel Claus-then William Caldwell, Sr., associate in arms in frontier forays, possibly was serving as the child's god-father, formally or informally. Certainly, in later years Captain Billy remained very close to and dependent on the Claus family. This was especially true of Billy's relationship with William Claus, who succeeded his father in the Indian Department. This Greeting to Young Master Caldwell also suggests that as an infant Billy was known as Thomas, which was a favored Caldwell family name, one that William, Sr., gave his third son by Suzanne Baby. The theme of abandonment also emerges from this birthday song the thoughtful Claus wrote for the small Caldwell child.

The lack of attention given Billy by his father is, in part, understandable, for the latter was an extremely preoccupied man in the years immediately before and following his eldest son's birth. Arriving in Virginia from County Fermanagh, in 1773, he enlisted with Lord Dunmore the next year, served in the Shawnee wars, and by 1776 had risen to the rank of company commander. That year his uncle James implored him to enlist in the rebel cause, but William held to his British loyalty and made his way to Niagara with a letter of recommendation to his cousin Lieutenant Colonel John Caldwell of the 8th Regiment. In 1777 he was commissioned senior captain in Butler's Ranger Corps, in which capacity he served, from Western New York to the Detroit frontier, until the end of the Revolutionary War. Perhaps the most active and effective of all John Butler's eight company commanders, Caldwell was rarely in garrison at Niagara-except when recuperating from wounds or illness. Near constantly engaged in patrols, raids, ambushes, and feints, he had little time or attention to give to the Mohawk woman from Joseph Brant's village with whom he had a passing liaison sometime between 1778 and 1780, nor much inclination to express concern for the son she bore him.[25]

In his eight years of military service in the colonies through the spring of 1782 William Caldwell at no time operated in association with any Potawatomi serving the British cause. The tribesmen who lived, traveled, and fought with him were drawn from the ranks of the Six Nations Iroquois, and Shawnee, Delaware, and Wendat communities in Pennsylvania and Ohio. Not until 1782 did Caldwell come close to the scene of Potawatomi activities. For this reason, the possibility of Billy Caldwell's having a mother from that tribe is precluded.[26] In April, 1782 Sir Frederick Haldimand ordered a ranger detachment dispatched to the Detroit frontier to counter a feared attack by George Rogers Clark. William Caldwell and his company were selected for this responsibility, and at this point the ranger leader departed the Niagara area forever, in process abandoning his young son and mother. It was Caldwell who, on his way west, led the combined British-Shawnee-Delaware-Wendat force that met and defeated Colonel William Crawford's advancing columns on the Upper Sandusky on June 4th. Severely wounded during the first shots of this engagement, the elder Caldwell was transported to Detroit, where he eventually settled.[27]

Little is known of Billy Caldwell's activities and involvements in the first decade of his life, except that he remained with his mother and her people in the Mohawk villages in the east. What this means is that Billy, as a boy, participated in the migrations and grave dislocations experienced by that tribe in the years following the Revolutionary War, when Joseph Brant had to remove his people from New York and resettle them along the Grand River north of Lake Ontario.[28] Meanwhile, in Detroit and vicinity, his father quickly accommodated himself to the shock of demobilization and the opportunities of peace. Soon he was engaged in business with Matthew Elliot, busy with land speculations, and developing his personal estate near present Amherstburg, Ontario. His clients and allies who settled nearby consisted of other disbanded rangers, partisan leaders from the late war, and the Canadian Wendat, a population with which the Caldwells sustained a close relationship for many years thereafter.

In 1783 William Caldwell, Sr., ignoring his Mohawk woman and son in the east, had taken to wife one Suzanne Baby, daughter of Duperon. In this fashion he allied himself with the powerful, wealthy, French-Canadian Baby kin-group. Shortly Suzanne began producing a series of sons and daughters for her husband, who was fully occupied increasing his own wealth, influence, and prestige. These developments, curiously, precipitated an awkward reunion between father William and his eldest son. Under the Law of Quebec that applied to such cases, this first-born child had first claim to his father's estate. A proper French bourgeoisie lady concerned with the rights of her own sons, it was Suzanne who insisted the threat be managed by bringing the boy west and incorporating him into the Caldwell household.

The exact dates of these developments are unknown; they lie in the years 1787 to 1791; and the boy, therefore, was between seven and eight years old. Somewhere in these years his father traveled to the Grand River, picked up his son, and brought him to Amherstburg. It was then that the person later known as Billy Caldwell properly arrived on the historical scene. When he arrived at the Caldwell home in Amherstburg he was a small, slender, preadolescent, monolingual Mohawk boy, and probably a very confused and distraught one at that. Abandoned by his father as an infant, while a growing child-one fully socialized into a Mohawk community, he was transported out of the membership groups familiar to him into an alien-and not especially receptive-social milieu, in process being abandoned again, this time by his mother and her people.[29] For a child this age such experiences are sufficient to stifle the developing sense of trust in others, to foster ambivalence and dependency, to incubate an expectation of defeat during controversies with larger and stronger persons, and to produce an inordinate need for recognition.[30] Thus, before puberty, Caldwell's eldest son was forced to surrender one growing sense of ego-identity and to relinquish the anchor points of his early life, those significant persons in the Mohawk community who had provided him with the norms, values, and skills that had given meaning to his first years.

Once incorporated into the Caldwell household he became known as Billy, a name that remained with him the rest of his life. This diminutive tag reflected the boy's status in his new family relationships-second in line to his younger half-brothers who were the favored targets of their father's largess. His step mother insisted he be raised Catholic, and he remained true to this religion until his death, while his father sent him to school with his other sons. There he acquired a "fair plain education...," that is, he learned ciphering, became literate and fluent in English, and mastered a simple, clumsy, trader's French. Although some of his Mohawk mannerisms remained with him, he soon lost the capacity to use his natal language. In later years only when he was in a state of diminished consciousness did evidence of his early linguistic socialization show through in his correspondence enough to interfere with his generally firm control of English syntax and his pretentious prose style. As he grew older he acquired a minor reputation as a juvenile delinquent among the merchants in Detroit, while evidence of some sibling jealousy seeps through the scanty records for this period. His brother, James, for example, characterized him as "naturally smart (i.e. likable)" and noted that he "received many presents from whites in consequence."[31] Billy was in process of developing an interpersonal style that was to mark his relationships most of his adult years: he tended to fawn upon and to ingratiate himself with the powerful, presenting himself as a loyal, dutiful, subordinate. However, this demeaning posture he would not assume within his own family group. His father planned for him a career in the Anglo-Irish squirearchy's tradition for dealing with bastard sons: Billy was to become manager of the family plantation. But this diminished status Billy would not and did not have to accept, for other opportunities lay ready at hand.

    Once settled at Amherstburg Billy Caldwell had to fashion a new, situation-appropriate concept of himself. What emerged was a composite of the elements and models provided by neighbors and kin. Put behind him was his Mohawkness, to emerge in later years only as a small emotional cancer, a despised and submerged fragment of himself, an element of self-doubt which occasionally plagued him. In the Detroit-Sandwich (now Windsor) region this decade-ending 1797-was full of the bustle of commerce, political maneuver, international confrontations and negotiations, divided and opposed loyalties, tribal movements, and border war. During these years Billy introjected as part of his own identity the sterling virtues of this frontier-a market mentality, loyalty to kin, economic independence, hard work, time-mindedness, the acceptance of his place in an emerging hierarchical class system, and unswerving obedience to constituted authority whether the informal influence of a patron or the power of formal national office holder. Before the decade ended Billy defined himself as a good Catholic, an Anglo-Irishman, and a loyal British subject. In 1797, faced with the choice of remaining attached to his father's household as a second-class son and family retainer or seeking his own fortune elsewhere, he opted for a measure of self-autonomy. Like many other Anglo-Irishmen of his age and era, he crossed the frontier by apprenticing himself in the fur-trade and entered into the wilderness.

That year Captain Billy engaged himself to Robert and Thomas Forsyth, who were then in process of moving their operations southward from L'Arbre Croche. By 1803 he had advanced to the position of clerk with the newly combined Forsyth-John Kinzie firm in the tiny post at Chicago. The next year, now operating temporarily as an independent, he first met Alexander Robinson near present Niles, Michigan. Later that year, in company with his younger half-brother, William Caldwell, Jr., he began trading in the Wabash River valley. Soon thereafter he was again affiliated with the Forsyths and Kinzies in the Illinois country, and this relationship continued strong for another thirty years. Although Billy saw himself as a self-managing, independent trader in these early years, it is clear that had again gotten himself entangled with men far stronger and more competent than himself. The Forsyths and Kinzies never allowed Billy to neglect how they defined the relationship. These imperious, single-minded men saw Billy as a client, their man, an object to serve their interests and to bend to their will. In freeing himself from his father's household and control, Billy Caldwell had injected himself into a relationship that sustained, promoted, and depressed him until the last years of his life.[32]

It was in their villages along the St. Joseph River that Captain Billy began his long association with the Potawatomi. Following the "custom of the country" and the model set by his father, there he took his first wife. She was a Potawatomi girl called La Nanette, indicating she was baptized Catholic, and the daughter of Wabinema ("White Sturgeon") and niece to the notorious Neskotnemek, better known as "Mad Sturgeon." Marriage to her provided Billy with an entree and an alliance with the large and powerful Fish clan. Following La Nanette's death Billy remarried, at Chicago this time, Robert Forsyth's daughter by an Ojibwa woman, a marriage that solidified his relationship with the increasingly influential Forsyth-Kinzie network. This girl died in child-bed soon after the wedding, and Billy's next wife was a French woman. Together, Billy's first three wives gave him some eight to ten children, none of whom survived him, including the tragic Alexander who died in 1832 sodden with drink in the streets of early Chicago. In these marriages we can trace a clear record of Billy's developing political and economic alliances, and one of upward mobility in the crude class-structure of the region.33 Something of his painful disappointments with his own children are revealed in a newsy letter to his brother Francis in 1834 when Billy wrote, "My son Alex came home last Thursday, all most naked, I have not said anything to him yet, about his future conduct.... whether he will be a vagrant, or reform for the better...while writing this my daughter Elizabeth six years of age [lies] on the point of death...thank God she was Baptiste (sic) by Father Badin...Remember to all our relatives, so adieu."34

Only the broad outlines of Caldwell's activities between 1803 and the spring of 1812 are known. In these years he established himself in his adult work role as an Indian trader, provided for his growing family, hewed to his Catholic religion, continued his relationship as client serving the Forsyth-Kinzie interests, further developed his influence among the Potawatomi, Ojibwa, and Odawa living around the southern end of Lake Michigan, and maintained his identification with and affection for the Caldwell family in Upper Canada. By the summer of 1812 he had emerged as a well established cultural broker, but a subordinate one. At that moment in his life larger political events converged, sweeping him toward a position of importance he had never previously enjoyed. As an established Indian trader of ambiguous national allegiance, particularly one reputed to be influential among the powerful and inveterately hostile, anti-American Potawatomi, his loyalties were a prize coveted in both Amherstburg and Vincennes.

Sometime in early summer, 1812, Billy's patron, John Kinzie, stabbed and killed a competitor, John LaLime, outside the gate of Fort Dearborn. Fearful of the legal consequences of this deed, Kinzie dispatched Caldwell to serve as his agent, interceding on his behalf with Governor William Henry Harrison at the territorial capital of Vincennes. Upon his arrival there Billy found the Americans anticipating a declaration of war and busy marshalling their too scanty resources. These officials immediately set to work in a foredoomed effort to enlist Billy in their cause. In a letter written four years after these events to his old friend, William Claus, Billy himself narrated his experiences in Vincennes. The occasion was a maudlin, self-justifying letter to his patron, Claus, written just after Caldwell learned he was to be discharged from the British Indian Department following four years of faithful service. The Americans offered him a "very high salary...to remain in the Indian country to keep the Indians neutral," he said, together with privileged trade concession there. But, he commented, he had "too great a share of true principal" to accept this offer. To have done so would have required him to abandon the staunch position he had long taken as a true Briton and a loyal Indian trader among the western tribes as well as recommendations he had been giving these tribesmen. They, too, he had long counseled, should hold fast to their British allegiance against the Americans.35 Seemingly faced with a major decision and a large opportunity, Billy had no real option. His decision had been made years before he had been elected to sustain himself with the personal identity of a fully committed Briton. His years spent amidst the United Empire Loyalist community at Amherstburg had left their enduring mark.

In some secondary accounts of Billy's trip to Vincennes Governor Harrison is made to conceal the news of the declaration of war from Billy and to keep him under house arrest. Upon learning of the outbreak of war, Billy is supposed to have escaped and made his way to the Detroit frontier. There, he rejoins Tecumseh, whom he had allegedly long served as personal secretary, and he leads his Potawatomi warriors across the border. Thereupon, he is noted as participating in the defense of Fort Malden against the abortive American invasion of the Ontario Peninsula, as well as in skirmishes on the American shore at Brownstown and Monguagua, August 5 and 9, 1812. However, these accounts do not coincide with each other, documented facts and Billy's own version of his experiences during this period.36

The American Congress did not declare war until June 18th, while Governor Harrison left the territorial capital the next day to rejoin his family in Cincinnati, long before receiving any word of this development, and he did not return for many weeks. In Captain Billy's own account of this period, he placed himself five hundred miles from Amherstburg when he received news of the war, and he made no mention of being detained by or escaping from Harrison.[37] Indeed, on July 15th, about when news of the war is known to have reached the area, Caldwell is documented as conducting business as usual at the Kinzie-Forsyth emporium in Peoria. At that time he was still John Kinzie's clerk, not Tecumseh's personal secretary. Tecumseh is known to have had a preference for traditional verbal communications and a profound aversion for the sons of Euro-American men by tribal women. Had he employed Billy Caldwell as his secretary in the five years after 1807, then surely some message written in Billy's distinctive hand would have survived in the Canadian or American archives; but no such document is known to exist. Moreover, in the fall of 1815, Caldwell indicated in a letter to Duncan Cameron that the first battle in which he served the British cause occurred in January 1813. This was the fight at the River Raisin, where Billy was severely wounded by one of General Winchester's officers whom he was attempting to rescue. The legend that he had enjoyed an especially close relationship with Tecumseh apparently was initiated by Billy Caldwell, himself, many years after that Shawnee leaders' death on the banks of the Thames River. In this wise he was obviously joining the multitude of Americans, Britons, and Canadians who, after the Treaty of Ghent, polished their egos by inventing or exaggerating a relationship with Tecumseh.[38]

Caldwell's presence in Peoria on July 15 places him just eighty miles south and thirty days shy of the bloody events at Chicago on August 15, 1812. There, on that date, the assembled Potawatomi finally gathered up their courage to assault the exposed and vulnerable garrison of Fort Dearborn. Mrs. Kinzie's overly glorified version of Billy's supposed participation in the aftermath of these happenings are generally discounted, as is much of the balance of her narrative. Given the standard assumptions concerning Caldwell, such a judgement is understandable. It does not strain credibility for a "Potawatomi chief," one then firmly attached to the British interest, even one coached by Tecumseh, to have intervened so as to rescue an odd-lots group of hapless "white survivors." However, Billy Caldwell was not then perceived by others as a Potawatomi "chief," nor did he so define his role, nor had he yet formally enlisted in the British service.

Recognizing Billy Caldwell's statuses and roles for what they were at the time at least makes the possibility of his appearance and intervention basically credible. He had long standing, general influence among many Potawatomi of Michigan, Indian, and Illinois. The organizer of the attack, <u>Neskotnemek</u>, was-by Potawatomi reckoning-Billy's father-in-law, through his earlier marriage to La Nanette. This gave him a particular claim on the attention of key personnel. The Kinzies, further, were not simply Caldwell's "good white friends." On the contrary, John Kinzie was Billy's employer of many years standing; and Billy was generally loyal to all who enjoyed his services. Moreover, many years later and in separate statements, both Alexander Robinson and William Caldwell, Jr., asserted that Billy had arrived in Chicago in time to assist the Kinzies. Neither of these men was eye-witness to the event, and both likely got the information from Captain Billy, himself. The fact that in his own narrative of 1820 John Kinzie made no mention of Caldwell's presence blocks any conclusion concerning his participation. But Kinzie was not a forgiving man, and shortly after the destruction of Fort Dearborn's garrison Billy deserted his employ, called eastward by older and stronger loyalties, absenting himself for some eight years. In 1820, when Kinzie described his family's rescue, Billy Caldwell had not yet returned from his unsuccessful attempt at establishing himself as a person of worth in Upper Canada, and, so, at that point, his relations with the Kinzies and Forsyths remained unmended.39

Sometime in the fall or early winter of 1812-1813, Billy Caldwell made his way to Amherstburg. The details of this journey, and how he disposed of his then living wife and children, are undocumented. He must have gone anticipating but he did not actually obtain a warm reception from his father and siblings. As the war approached William Caldwell, Sr., had worked to create an appropriate place for himself and his sons in its preparations. He hoped and schemed to organize an independent corps of frontier rangers under his personal command, one modeled after John Butler's force in which he has served so effectively during the Revolutionary War. Not until January, 1813 was his plan approved by Colonel Henry Proctor, although Caldwell, his sons, and his neighbors had been operating with the 1st Essex Militia before that date. After the formation of "Caldwell's Rangers" was approved, the old man secured captaincies for his sons Wiliam and Thomas, and a commission as Ensign for his younger son Francis. Billy

Caldwell, however, was not a recipient of his father's patronage. Upon arriving in Amherstburg he once more experienced paternal rejection and had to locate his own place in the war effort. Capitalizing on his influence among the western tribes, he soon obtained for himself the rank of Captain in the paramilitary Western Division of the British Indian Department. In this capacity Captain Billy Caldwell served throughout the war and well into the post-war years, first in cooperation with the Right and later with the Center Division of the British forces in Upper Canada. His duties generally carried him to the same sectors of operations in which his father and brother were fighting and promoting their careers. Throughout the war Billy served side by side in the Indian Department with his close friend, an old companion of the Wabash River trading days and a fellow Anglo-Irishman, Captain John Wilson.40

Captain Billy's first combat experience with the Indian Department was in January, 1813, as he himself noted. Later that year he participated in Proctor's unsuccessful siege of Fort Meigs, and he cowered in a ditch under heavy fire from the guns of Fort Stephenson. Following Perry's naval victory at Put-in-Bay, he joined in the general British retreat up the valley of the Thames River, and he was at the scene of the battle when Tecumseh was killed at Moravian Town. Like everyone else involved, he later embellished his participation that day, polishing his public image with the claim he had seen Tecumseh shot. From Moravian Town Billy, in company with other officers of the Indian Department, shepherded the few remaining western Indians toward the British defensive lines at Burlington Beach. There were, then, few Potawatomi remaining in Upper Canada-most had already deserted their fleeing ally and made their way back to Michigan. Once in the British positions on Lake Ontario Billy continued his services to the department. His most notable military exploit in 1814 involved a successful raid on American positions near Niagara. But events were shaping up for a more personally significant domestic and departmental battle.41

In the spring of 1814 Billy involved himself in the first of two recorded acts of attempted administrative patricide. The setting for the first-an abortive-assault on his father's position included the long-standing dispute between regular officers of the British army and civil authorities over control of the personnel and functioning of the quasi-military Indian

Department. This smoldering controversy was complicated by further involvement in a conflict between the Grand River Iroquois and everyone else in the Canadas. Captain Billy's first attempt on his father's position was precipitated by the terminal illness and later death of Matthew Elliot, then Deputy Superintendent General of Indian Affairs for the western division. In the squabble over selection of a successor for Elliot, Billy found himself allied with the army against civil authorities, with the Mohawk against his father and the Indian Department, and with a combine of younger officers in the department against their superiors, particularly his father. In public Billy remained openly deferential, respectful, obedient, and loving in communications to or concerning his father. Covertly, he was acting out long submerged resentments as well as expressing his own personal ambitions.[42]

William Caldwell, Sr., was the obvious political choice as successor to his old partner Matthew Elliot, if Sir John Johnson and William Claus were to maintain their administrative integrity and freedom in decision making in their department. But the elder Caldwell, who in the past decade had run a poor second to Elliot's performance, was obviously growing inept in his duties. Like Elliot he was an aged man, his faculties failing him, on the edge of becoming obsolete in a fast changing social environment. Unlike Elliot, he had not demonstrated himself an effective manager of men and resources so far during the war. Indeed, at the time of Elliot's death Caldwell was behaving ineptly in a controversy over the distribution of Indian supplies and presents with Major John Norton-the sometime Cherokee-Scot, later British Army private and deserter, then protege of Joseph Brant, and by 1814 a compelling, Bryonic figure much favored by the British aristocracy and army as well as recognized leader of the Mohawk.

Billy's aspirations in the combination against his father were exposed once news of Elliot's incapacitating, final illness spread. At that moment Billy was serving a Major Dean as liaison between the few hundred western Indians he controlled and the army. About April 26, bypassing the chain-of-command in the Indian Department, Dean issued garrison orders appointing Billy Acting Deputy Superintendent General and instructed him to take up Elliot's duties. To these orders Captain Caldwell quickly assented, while at the same time striving to conceal the tracks of his machinations from view by his superiors in the Indian Department. For some days he worked at assuming his new duties, but without the cooperation of those who might have validated the appointment. Then William Claus and Sir John Johnson moved, ignoring the army's action, asserting their legal authority, and officially replaced the now deceased Elliot with Billy's father, Lt. Colonel William Caldwell. Thus Billy's ambitions were temporarily thwarted, although his involvement in the continuing conspiracy against his father went on. The substance of the charges against the elder Caldwell were revealed in an unsigned letter, one likely written by Matthew Elliot, Jr., that December. In this letter the writer detailed a variety of complaints from sundry individuals about Colonel Caldwell, identified Matthew Elliot, Jr., John Wilson, and George Ironside as aligned against him, and specified that their first choice as a superior was Billy Caldwell. Among the allegations in this letter was the claim that Colonel Caldwell's ineptitude had nearly caused Billy to lose his treasured influence among the western Indians, and the-accurate-assertion that he was appointing his sons Wiliam, Thomas, and Francis to offices (and salaries) in the department threatening the positions of the complainants.43

This dismal episode left relations between father and son sorely strained, a matter exacerbated by the fact that Colonel Caldwell was now also Captain Billy Caldwell's commanding officer. In June Billy was in command of a successful raiding party against American positions near Lewistown, his last military exploit under British auspices. Then, as the American units operating in the Ontario Peninsula founds their lines of communication threatened and retreated west of the Detroit River, the Indian Department was instructed to support the army's occupation of that border. Captain Billy was the officer selected by his father for this undesirable responsibility, but Billy managed never to get himself or his few Indian charges on the move. Colonel Caldwell, in his turn, busied himself promoting an absurd scheme to reduce the costs of Indian administration by moving all the western Indians then in the Canadas west to the Mississippi River by their forcing a passage a passage through Michigan, where they might, hopefully, disrupt American activities. The Indians-then returned at some five hundred combat age if not combat ready men, outnumbered a hungry six to one by their women and children and their sick, wounded, and aged, would have none of this. They, in their turn, were quietly participating in truce negotiations with William Henry Harrison, making inordinate demands on the British Indian Department, playing one branch of same off against another so as to double their rations, and issuing half-promises to their masters which they had neither the power nor the inclination to keep. Meanwhile, Billy remained, on the surface, a dutifully respectful son, solicitous of his father's health and general well-being.[44]

That winter Captain Billy was involved in a peculiar incident revealing another side of his personality. The time had come for Brigadier General Henry Proctor's court martial for his failures during 1813. Desperate for testimony on his behalf, he called upon Billy Caldwell as a defense witness. Billy responded affirmatively and spent twenty days in Montreal during December and January, 1814 and 1815, in support of Proctor's case. Then, in an obvious quid pro quo, Billy called upon Proctor for a testimonial as to his conduct during the war, and on March 1 was delivered a glowing commendation. Calling on Proctor at that time for a letter of recommendation was, at best, aberrant, for the general's career was shattered, and he stood badly disgraced. Billy was making an oddly inept choice for a character witness, while displaying little regard for Proctor's sensitivities by demanding his modest reward for services rendered.[45]

During the spring of 1815 Billy was an ambivalent participant in the second, this time successful, attack on his father's position. In the end he wound up temporarily occupying his father's office, but this controversy brought him grave attacks of conscience, acute depression, and no lasting job security. Billy departed the British positions on Lake Ontario on May 11 for Amherstburg, preceded a few days by his father. Before departing, in a letter to Duncan Cameron, he parroted the Indian Department's sentiments about an unusually short-fused officer, Lieutenant Colonel Reginald James, whom he characterized as "that brute." Within a few months Billy would find Colonel James his ally, if an extremely painful one. James was placed in command of the military detachments near Amherstburg, and before leaving for the west he and William Caldwell, Sr., had been involved in an acrimonious public dispute. Throughout the ensuing episode Billy remained in very high favor in the Indian Department, particularly in the eyes of his patron, William Claus. In May, for example, Claus argued that as the war ended he would have to keep Captain Billy Caldwell and his good friend John Wilson on the pay list at Amherstburg so as to sustain some influence among the western Indians, who were being successfully courted by the Americans. Claus much favored Billy over Captains Matthew Elliot, Jr., and Alexander McKee, Jr . the young and ill-experienced sons of illustrious fathers by Shawnee women. In these circumstances Billy was ordered west, as an ambitious second-in-command to his father.46

Billy Caldwell arrived on the Detroit River in late May and quickly settled into his work. He was soon faced with the difficult tasks of re-establishing the post at Amherstburg, disposing of the western Indians still in British territory, and developing peaceful working relationships with his American counterparts across the uneasy international border. His father remained in nominal command and held tight to the reins of administrative authority, but his private interests and failing health forced him to delegate most of the responsibility to his subordinates, especially Billy, whom he treated with arbitrary and contemptuous formality.47 Relations between William Caldwell, Sr., and Colonel James, never comfortable, steadily worsened. James characterized the elder Caldwell as an "insubordinate imbecile," while Caldwell similarly expressed his regard by calling James a "petty martinet." Throughout this growing dispute and the remaining months of his father's tenure in office Billy walked a narrow, obstacle strewn path. To his father he was formally correct; in his communications with superiors in the Indian Department he echoed prevailing sentiments about the difficulties of dealing with the British military; but he remained polite and suitably deferential to the one man who was the mover and shaker in the whole affair, Lieutenant Colonel Reginald James.48

Colonel James kept up the pressure on William Caldwell, Sr., through the summer and fall of 1815. In late July he stage-managed a delegation of tribal leaders, who planned to travel east to York (present Toronto), there to present their complaints against Caldwell to the ranking military officials. Among the dignitaries who made this journey was Tecumseh's brother, Tenskatawa, formerly known as the Prophet, now styling himself the "Shawnee King." Rapidly slipping in prestige and influence in the post-war environment, Tenskatawa was then making himself into a source of petty annoyance to British officialdom. Caldwell, Sr., intervened with the demand that his son, William, Jr., accompany the delegation as guide and interpreter, but Colonel James rejected this proposal out of hand and proposed his nominee for this responsibility, Caldwell's eldest son, Billy. Their compromise candidate was Lieutenant Gravesett, the Commissary officer.[49] William Caldwell, Sr., was unable successfully to fend off this barrage of attacks from James, while by now Captain Billy had been made painfully uncomfortable by his part in the affair. The multiple public and private conflicts engendered by the dispute were proving too much for him. Kowtowing to James in their face-to-face meetings, he berated him in private letters to his seniors in the Indian Department. Suffering from his father's displeasure, he continued to express a sense of profound need for his family's acceptance and recognition.

By late August, then close to emotional breakdown, Captain Billy had become addicted to a patent medicine compounded of brandy and laudanum, one dispensed in a bottle labeled "Jesuit's Drops." Apparently the opiate of the Indian Department, it was a powerful depressant. Under the influence of this potion, on August 28th Billy drafted a letter pouring out his troubles to one of the three men in whom he could safely confide, Duncan Cameron, secretary to William Claus. In these nearly indecipherable pages Captain Billy made one of his extremely rare, and a most revealing, comment on his Indianness. "I will continue to trouble you with my moodiness," (sic) he wrote his confidant, "until you say you will not be troubled by any more of of my Indian importunity." The submerged fragment of Billy's identity that he thought of as Indian was dependency, specifically claims upon the attention and favors of others more powerful then himself. "Our troubles [are] commencing a pies (apace)," he continued, "Commissariat Bully (Lieutenant Gravesett) arrived yesterday with his Prosytites [Prostitutes, i.e., the Indian delegation from Kingston very proud of their mission below...They never surrendered their thoughts to me...Lieutenant Gravesett have not thought worth his while to report to the Supt. General [Colonel Caldwell-in fact [he is a] second Norton all through the influence of Colonel James." Billy went on to mock the war records of the tribal leaders who had gone east. The Shawnee King for example, he thought "not worth his salt as a soldier." He concluded, "but why should I trouble myself with people that I hardly ever saw in a battle with me...and I have not mist (sic) a Battle since January 1812 [actually, 1813]...which I had the Honor of acting in cooperation with the Right Division."[50]

The entire situation came to a head on October 21. That date the imperious Colonel James seized the opportunity the elder Caldwell had presented by refusing him the services of an interpreter and summarily discharged the Assistant Deputy Superintendent General. In a District Order promulgated on the same day, James appointed Captain Billy in his father's stead. The following day all participants settled into their offices to initiate a stream of letters to each other and to their superiors and supporters. Belatedly recognizing his error, the senior Caldwell moved to provide Colonel James the interpreter he had been ordered to deliver earlier. James would have none of this: his decision was final. Both James and William Caldwell wrote their superiors justifying their conduct and castigating each other. Captain Billy, at last in a position he had hoped for, was not elated. Indeed, he had William Claus's judgement of his conduct to consider, and he remained depressed. On the 22nd he wrote Colonel James in a condescending tone, accepting the responsibilities and orders issued him. He concluded, in reference to his father's conduct, "I am going to say a few minutes of reflection would [have] avoided so disagreeable [a] contention. It is not to Palliate the conduct of any Officer belonging to his majesty's service."[51]

On the other hand, that same day, he wrote Duncan Cameron, secretary to his patron and legitimate superior in the Indian Department, William Claus. "The long promised explosion, have at last arrived," he observed, then proceeded to outline the happenings in a straightforward fashion that did no justice to his father's case. In this letter, as in later correspondence, he referred to his father as the "ADSG of Indian Affairs," as if he were no more than a former superior and their family relationship had been severed. Billy thereupon occupied himself with the conduct of his duties as the new Acting Deputy Superintendent of Amherstburg; however, his tenure in office was insecure. Indeed, there was then less than a year remaining before he, in turn, was to be discharged.[52]

Billy's security was threatened by more than the fact that he had demonstrated a certain opportunism and-especially critical in a year that civil authorities were reasserting their exclusive power in Indian affairs-an inability to deal effectively with the British military. A period of sharp economizing in British Indian administration was then beginning, and older, wiser, better experienced men than he, Indian Department officers with patrons more influential than Billy's were waiting in line for the few remaining salaried positions. Nonetheless, William Claus-who himself was then losing his grip-continued to offer Captain Billy whatever favor he could. Claus obviously perceived Billy as Billy wished himself to be seen, as the lamenting son of a sadly wronged father.

On November 10, assuming the part of a benevolent godparent as much as that of a superior, Claus wrote Billy advising him that he was working to control the conflict and secure justice for his department. Claus advised Billy not to allow the troubles with his father at Amherstburg to get the better of him, adding, "but do your duty in every point and be above that dirty jealousy that appears to possess the minds of some people. I have every confidence in your prudence." A week later Duncan Cameron advised Billy that senior military officers in Montreal had approved Colonel James's firing of his father, while rejecting Billy's appointment and substituting Lieutenant Colonel William McKay. Claus immediately blocked this additional intervention into departmental affairs by ordering McKay, who was his subordinate, to report to Drummond island, then the Antarctica of the Indian Department. In this fashion, with the able support of old patrons, Billy remained, over the winter of 1815-1816, temporarily in command of Indian affairs at Amherstburg.[53]

That winter Claus visited Amherstburg to investigate affairs at the post, where he determined that William Caldwell, Sr., was indeed incompetent and that he could do nothing further to support him. But on a larger scene he was successful in securing agreement from the military on a policy of non-interference in Indian affairs.[54] Captain Billy was doing little to further his own case, for he was half derelict in his duties, particularly as regards furnishing Claus with the returns, receipts, certificates, and journals that hard pressed officer badly needed to defend his department in a period of increased economy in Indian affairs. Although Billy remained in nominal command until the following October 24, his activities were increasingly scrutinized and supervised by both the military and the man who was his official subordinate, the post storekeeper, a far better experienced, well educated heir to Matthew Elliot-the older George Ironside, Sr.[55]

By last April, 1816, Captain Billy had been made fully aware his fortunes had ebbed.. On the 27th of that month he scrawled the draft of another drunken maudlin, self-justifying, self-revealing letter, this one addressed but never actually mailed to William Claus. He had already demonstrated he had not accepted Claus's paternal advice to go quietly about his duties in every detail. In this letter he revealed he was also obsessed by that "dirty jealousy" Claus had strongly warned him against. He acknowledged that George Ironsides was de facto superintendent, but belittled this older mans capabilities. He next launched into a lengthy history of the failings of British Indian policy and praised himself for what he, as a loyal Indian trader, had done to support the true interests of his nation, Great Britain. He allowed himself a few half-threatening remarks: "What I have stated in this is not with a view to look for Bread," he wrote, "but merely to put you in mind of a future day, as you are Head of the Dept..."He called for some departmental patronage for his special friends, Captain John Wilson and Lieutenant Edward Sayer, and launched a tirade against his rivals, particularly the "half Dutch Langlade." After accusing Colonel James of sundry peculations, he concluded with the remark, "Sir, if I was party again to 1811 and know as much as I know now...I suffer you I would take care of my own affairs and not enter into political affairs again." But this outright rejection of his values and nationality were too much for the badly conflicted Billy Caldwell. Thus, he added, "but why should I pet (fret?) about what cannot be recalled...if I am in the province and war was to break out I would surely turn out again, for my principle is not, in the least impaired by the last wounds received."[56]

At this point in his career it is evident the only leverage Captain Billy enjoyed with British officials was his reputed influence among the western (i.e., United States) tribesmen, which was increased in value by the concern of administrators in Upper Canada with their still uncomfortable relations across the Great lakes border with Americans. However, the Indian Department had ben enjoined to move all remnants of the western tribesmen back to their homes in the United States where they might conceivably serve British interests without the expense of having to feed them daily. In this context Billy's supposed influence carried no lasting weight at all. Indeed, he was being gently eased out of his position in a fashion that would cause the least disturbance, and he displayed neither the integrity nor sufficient good sense to resign his position while still in official good standing. During the summer of 1816 and the following winter Caldwell's position fell from misfortune toward calamity, eventually reaching such a low as would four years later, drive him away from the groups whose esteem he most treasured, his family, the Indian Department, and his friends in Canada.

It is in view of these reduced circumstances that Captain Billy's testimony for his Potawatomi-Odawa client Shabni ("He Has Pawed Through"), can be properly interpreted. This document, generally seen as testimony that Caldwell had joined Tecumseh in 1807, actually asserted that it was Shabni who then allied himself with the Shawnee brothers. Here Billy Frenchified Shabni's name, making it Chamblee, as he often did with both English and Potawatomi words. What Billy was doing in writing this pass or testimonial was bolstering his own self esteem by dispensing what small favors and patronage he yet controlled, as he attempted to do in this period for several of his other associates from the War of 1812.[57]

Captain Billy's decline continued in the summer and fall of 1816. Although he remained on the job, John Askin, Jr., transferring to a warmer climate from Drummond Island, was appointed superintendent at Amherstburg. Askin never actually assumed his duties, and on October 27 George Ironsides, Sr., was formally named to the post he had unofficially assumed months earlier, whereupon Billy Caldwell was discharged from the Indian service. Billy's hated rivals, the Langlades, Rapps, Cadottes, and Gravesetts, were kept on at the reduced rank of interpreter. Lest it be concluded that Billy was being subjected to some sort of racial discrimination because of his "half-breed" status, it must be emphasized that the Amherstburg establishment was, simply, handed over to the survivors of the old Revolutionary War frontier elite and their descendents, especially the heirs to Matthew Elliot's influence. Moreover, at no time in Billy's career in the Indian Service was the status of his mother ever mentioned in official records or correspondence, nor was he ever stigmatized as "Indian" or "half-breed." Indeed, the men who replaced Billy in office or who remained on the payroll at Amherstburg were of precisely the same maternal antecedents as Billy himself. John Askin, Jr., for example, was the son of an Odawa woman, while George Ironsides, Jr., who replaced his retired father a decade later, was the son of a Mohawk daughter of Co-Co-Chee, born in a town on the Maumee River well described by Helen Tanner in her companion paper. Billy was removed from his position for reasons that will now be entirely clear: he was a man whose aspirations far outreached his capacities. He had not demonstrated himself adequate to the task of managing Indian affairs in the altered post-war climate. He had, moreover, grossly offended his father, who had himself been stripped of office and rank, and who was, therefore, neither in a position nor disposed to aid his eldest son.[58]

Captain Billy did not quickly or easily surrender his goal of establishing himself as a "true Briton" in Upper Canada. He spent the next four years striving to find some position that would provide him the economic security and recognition he craved. These years he lived in the vicinity of Amherstburg. He was unsuccessful in his efforts to obtain a half-pay pension for his services during the war; but with the aid of his friend John Wilson acting as his agent in Montreal, he did finally receive his unpaid allowances and the prize money for his raid on Lewiston.[59] Never in good spirits, his addiction to Jesuit's Drops continued. He engaged in a modest land speculation, which failed. He petitioned and obtained certificates for a Prince Regent's land grant, which was part of his reward as a wounded, serving officer during the war; but he obtained no benefits from this as he signed his certificates over to friends before departing Canada and they never delivered the proceeds of the sale to him. Finally, in 1818, he moved out of Amherstburg to the "New Settlement" at Colchester on the Lake Erie shore, where he engaged himself in a trading venture.[60]

During 1818 Captain Billy suffered two fresh wounds, perhaps more painful than any he had previously known. In January of that year three old cronies gathered around the aging and failing William Caldwell, Sr., to witness his last will and testament, and the final degradation of his eldest son. In this document, the old warrior handed his considerable estate over to his children by Suzanne Baby, while disinheriting Billy. He skillfully blocked any possibility of Billy's challenging the will by awarding him a valueless, undocumented, suspect title to an undescribed parcel of land on the Upper Thames River. Later that year, on July 28, Billy's old patron, William Claus, responded to an earlier plea to aid his fellow subordinate in obtaining half-pay with the advice that he no longer enjoyed any influence, and that he could not, or would not, provide any further assistance. In the following spring, 1819, Billy's venture in Colchester went bankrupt, and he found himself unemployed and penniless. At that point the record of Captain Billy's activities in Upper Canada ends. How he spent the next twelve months is undocumented and unremarked. However, sometime during 1820, by a route that is as obscure as the one he took upon traveling to Amherstburg eight years earlier, he moved himself and his family back to Chicago, once again seeking the patronage of John Kinzie and Thomas Forsyth, searching for an opportunity to make his mark that had escaped him during his ventures in the Canadas.61

In appraising Captain Billy's later career in Chicago and the west it is useful to recall that this was his second journey into American territory in search of better opportunity and meaning for his life, and it may be equally useful to remark that the United States was, for him, a very clear second choice as a national peg upon which he could hang his personal identity. Thus Billy traveled toward Chicago as a lapsed Briton. The judgement about his career as an American made many years later by his brother, William Caldwell, Jr., has to it the ring of partial truth. His opinion of Billy mellowed by the years, William noted that after the war he was "greatly coveted and favored by the American government. Indeed, they showed him greater favors against whom he fought, than the British government for whom he had so stoutly contended." William added that "Billy Caldwell was a man of fine business capacity...was made agent for the Americans against the Potawatomies," and he concluded with a misconception that was to enthrall the Canadian Caldwells for half a century after Billy's death, "he owned a large portion of what is now Chicago."62 William's sentiments do not, of course, reflect the judgements of those who employed and benefited from his talents in the Chicago area, including those of the Potawatomi "against" whom William believed Billy served as an American controlled agent.

In these circumstances Billy arrived in Chicago, not identifiable as a Potawatomi "half-breed" out to mulct his people, but as a failed public administrator, the disinherited son of an entrepreneurial Irish-French Canadian family, an insolvent merchant, a man unsuccessful in the task of adapting himself to the stresses of peace in a community he had served capably in war. Caldwell was clearly a driven, ambitious, upwardly mobile, white collar sort-"He never worked," commented Alexander Robinson,"but was always a trader." He was forty years old when he arrived in Chicago, and he obviously began his life there by investigating the kind of reception he might receive and he possibilities for a future in an area where he had first sought a place for himself seventeen years earlier. What he discovered was a small village in a new state, a community on the verge of a period of massive, prolonged economic and social development. The well known outlines of his career after 1829 must take on a different significance when viewed in the light of these background interpretations.63

Arriving in the Lake Michigan area Captain Billy learned of a new development he likely had not anticipated, one that soon influenced his fortunes and eventually moulded his fate. This involved a culture-historical process that offered Caldwell short-term opportunity while it threatened long term deprivation. Beginning after the Treaty of Ghent a new variety of humankind began appearing in the region. As first noted in the articles of the 1817 Treaty of St. Mary's on the Maumee River, these people were denominated "Indians by blood or adoption." There is no evidence that many, if any, such were properly adopted following tribal custom. Nor was "Indian blood," that is, descent from some tribesman ancestor, really a prerequisite for actual classification of many such individuals. What really differentiated this new kind of "Indians" from others was the fact that they were the children of American traders, Indian agents, government officials, and other entrepreneurs, and the fact that lands given to them in treaty proceedings were, without further restrictions or safeguards, deeded in fee simple, which meant that these valuable parcels of real estate could immediately be put on the open market.64

The criteria defining the boundaries of ethnic groups in the Great lakes were, thus, rapidly changing, with the category of "Indian" being broadened to include whole groups that had not earlier been so designated. In psychological and economic terms the marginal value of being "Indian" was rising rapidly; while that of being, for example. French was dropping. Indeed, it was the long-resident, Catholic, French-speaking population of the area, then being eased out of their positions of economic and political power by swarms of Scots-Irish and Anglo-Saxons, who provided the largest contingents of persons to switch their ethnic status in this period. Seen in this fashion, one opportunity Billy Caldwell met in the Chicago of 1820 was that of resuscitating his long repressed Mohawkness, while the risk he had to face was that of forever being stigmatized as a "half-breed Indian." The fact that Billy did not become Mohawk again, and that he did identify himself as Potawatomi, or perhaps Shawnee or Wyandot, by "blood or adoption," illustrates and confirms this point nicely. American officials and entrepreneurs in the Chicago area never had any need of the services of a cooperative Mohawk since this tribe was not involved in any land cessions in that neighborhood.

Once settled in Chicago Captain Billy at first gave no indication he would move in the direction of becoming and "Indian." On the contrary, it was plain he wished to establish himself as an educated, broadly experienced, ambitious tradesman, one eager to become accepted in his new identity- that of a British immigrant in process of becoming a loyal American. Thus, in 1825, he was recommended as Justice of the Peace in Chicago, while the following year he worked as a merchant and an election commissioner.65 In 1827, accompanied by his old companion, Shabni, he performed minor services on an intelligence gathering mission during the Winnebago scare. During these same years he worked in association with the Forsyths, Kinzies, Wolcotts, and others in the Indian business, and so, by 1829, the possibility of his being converted into a trustworthy, influential "Indian" caught up with him. That year, in conjunction with negotiations for the Treaty of Prairie du Chien, his American patrons arranged for him to be identified as a Potawatomi Chief. In that part-time, temporary capacity he served them ably for some six years. His reward for services performed at the 1829 treaty grounds was a two-and-one-half section parcel of land on the Chicago River, the first of numerous payments he was to extract from Americans. In these same years he also worked to promote the establishment of a Catholic church in Chicago, and attempted to introduce formal education for Prairie Potawatomi children.66

The quality of Billy's relationships with his Scots-Irish patrons in Chicago, as well as evidence of some of the stresses he was feeling in his new and conflict-ridden role, are revealed in an exchange of correspondence between himself and Thomas Forsyth during 1832. In the spring of that year Billy addressed Forsyth in a curiously complicated letter, one in which he assumed several alternating identities. He opened with a submissive supplication for aid, advice, and information, in which he seems to associate himself emotionally with the Potawatomi. The role he played in these first paragraphs seems to have been that of a traditional Potawatomi Kiktowenene ("One Who Impersonates"). Americans generally identified such an actor as the Speaker or sometimes the Peace Chief of this tribe. That is, Billy at first addressed Forsyth as the spokesman expressing the sentiments of the Potawatomi in traditional style.

However, in the next lines Caldwell abruptly changed his manner and wrote to Forsyth as a confidant, in process exposing some of the doubts he was suffering at age fifty. "Oh how times is going," he mused, "When I look back I was a boy a short time ago, and now past 50 years...and have done nothing yet of manhood...when will it come...probably never to act the part which I was created for...or die the cowardly death of a Bonaparte. He odd (ought) to have died at Waterloo, then he would (have) lived in the Bosoms of the Braves..." Here Billy Caldwell clearly expresses a profound sense of personal impoverishment and a sense of stagnant incompletion. He sees himself as an exile, a man who will never accomplish what he wished for-to become a person of stature and renown.

Caldwell closes his letter to Forsyth in a third personal style, on a man-to-man basis, as an equal gossiping about the doings of mutual acquaintances and kinsmen, and of matters of joint interest, such as the development of a harbor and lighthouse at Chicago. And he added a postscript in yet a fourth manner, as a military man passing on to his superior a fragment of tactical intelligence-the Sioux and Menominee, he indicates, are preparing to attack the Sauk and Fox.[67]

Forsyth's response to Billy, in contrast, was all of a psychological piece-haughty, imperious, and demanding. Billy is addressed straightforwardly as an underling. Introducing one Hugh McGill who was to act as Forsyth's attorney in coming treaty negotiations, he is ordered to see to it that the Potawatomi make provision for paying Forsyth his due, and to ensure that McGill send Forsyth as much money as possible, Forsyth allows no ambiguity whatever in how he defines Caldwell's role-he is his agent brokering his relations with he Potawatomi.[68]

This exchange was in preparation for the Treaty of Chicago, completed in the fall of 1833. In these negotiations Billy Caldwell played a very prominent part both on behalf of his patrons and with respect to the interests of the Potawatomi. He was supposedly carrying out the narrow responsibilities emphasized later by his brother, William. Actually, in that year, his loyalties had already been compromised and his identity was taking on a new dimension.[69] By that time Billy was entirely too old, too experienced, and too dissatisfied to be long comfortable in the role of a compliant middleman serving the interests of a superior.

The strains Billy was feeling, his private definition of his role, and something of how he was handling the pressures on him are made evident in a letter to his brother Francis written a half-year after the Treaty of Chicago.[70] Unable to provide equal satisfaction to all those adversaries clamoring for a share of the booty at the treaty grounds, Billy had made some general enemies, while he had not entirely pleased his major patrons. Thus he stood accused of various crimes; misdemeanors, and disloyalties. "You have understandably heard various tales about me," he wrote Francis, "but, I am perfectly easy in my mind about those faults (and?) reports about me...I told you all that I would not be a political Indian any more than what would be of benefit to my red brethren...that is to take them over the Mississippi in order to draw them from this scene of destruction." Billy Caldwell was not deceiving himself about his ethnic status. Instead, events at the treaty had forced him over still another watershed in his identity. He understood perfectly well that he had assumed the position of "political Indian" for limited purposes. He was now claiming the right himself to decide just what those purposes might be. And now he had begun to define his role as a protector and defender of the interests of the Prairie Potawatomi. It was this role that he acted out the remaining seven years of his life. In employing Captain Billy as their broker the Kinzies and Forsyths had neglected to provide him the recognition, the security, and the sense of integrity required to sustain him in that position. The Potawatomi, in contrast, lured and welcomed him, offering him respect and admiration, their highest titles, and other rewards for the services he might provide them. At this moment in his career Billy Caldwell had become an intercultural broker turned around, his skills and loyalties captured by those he was supposed to exploit.

The next year, with his son Charles, Caldwell accompanied a delegation of Potawatomi leaders on a long journey inspecting their new lands west of the Mississippi. Located in the Platte Purchase, pressures from the state of Missouri did not allow these tribesmen to remain long in occupation of these fertile lands. However, aided by Caldwell, the band leaders were able to wrest further concessions from the United States before moving again, during 1837, to another reserve in the western part of Iowa. There the Prairie bands came immediately under sharp pressure from two directions. The population of Iowa was expanding rapidly and moving toward statehood, which would eventually dislocate these Potawatomi. In the same years a coalition of missionaries and traders from Illinois and Indiana had decided on the Osage River reserve in eastern Kansas as the final resting place for all Potawatomi, where they might be brought together in one location under their exclusive management. But the Prairie bands' leaders would have none of this, and with the help of Caldwell they resisted a new treaty and removal for an additional ten years. In his last years Billy Caldwell was pioneering a new role that would come into its own among the Potawatomi only after his death, that of a business agent. On behalf of his "red brethren," he was acting as contractor, administrator, advocate, advisor, and principal negotiator in their dealings with the United States. The esteem in which the <u>wkamek</u> held Billy is nicely recorded in 1839 remarks of old <u>Abtekizhek</u> ("Half Day"). Then pressed to agree to a treaty and to relocate his people, Half Day told Stephen watts Kearny that it would be Billy Caldwell who the next day deliver their final decision, adding, "should he sell this country for fifty cents we will be satisfied. I have done!"

On the other side of the conference table American agents were forming quite different views of Billy Caldwell during his last years. In 1837, for instance, Sub-agent John Dougherty castigated him as a "cunning, designing, dangerous, speculating, unprincipled, drunken spoilt character," noting that "the officers of the government have given him his present influence over the tribe," and recommending that "it should be taken from him without delay." Dougherty added that "he is exercising said influence against the American government secretly, though as fervently as he did during the last war." Dougherty concluded with, "he has I think no red blood in him, but is a red coat savage at heart of the first order, even educated in the school of the notorious General Proctor at the River Raisin." The last thrust was unkind a swell as untrue, for Captain Billy was badly wounded on the Raisin River while attempting to prevent a massacre.[71]

Once arrived at Trader's point, in present Council Bluffs, Caldwell constructed his last home and there settled with his fourth wife, a French lady, to enjoy his remaining years. His new community was a tiny post on a raw frontier, and there for the next few years he was clearly its most prominent, noteworthy citizen. There he played godfather to the few Catholic children, and there he provided the only hospitality received by Father Pierre De Smet, when that greatly confused missionary arrived in 1838 anticipating a welcome by several thousand, fervently Catholic Potawatomi. From Council Bluffs Billy Caldwell mailed off letters to friends and kinsmen, as well as to the Chicago daily Tribune, communicating with and defending old friends and enemies, even William Henry Harrison. Captain Billy welcomed the dragoon officers when they came by on their lonely patrols, and he offered the warmth of his home to his Potawatomi clients. In his last years he had, at last, achieved the position of prominence he had long coveted, as a relatively large and commanding figure in a very small and impressionable community.72

Captain Billy Caldwell, or, as he had likely been christened, Thomas Caldwell, passed over his final frontier on 27 September 1841. The priests had abandoned their small mission station some weeks earlier and so there was none to anoint him, to hear the final confession of his numerous sins, and thus to give him comfort..His was no masculine hero's death the Kansas Potawatomi invented for him many years later. Weakened by old wounds and his several addictions, made infirm by age, he died in a cholera epidemic. His children long dead, he was attended only by his last wife, who in turn did not long survive him, and by a few old Potawatomi friends. His final lucid moments and his last, dismal thought were witnessed by a visitor, one James Clarke, a faithful Wendat retainer of the Canadian Caldwell's sent west to pay the last respects of brothers and sisters by inquiring into the size and disposition of Billy's estate, particularly his large land holdings in Chicago.73

The first reactions to Captain Bill's death were mixed. Upon hearing this long hoped for news, D.D. Mitchell, Superintendent at St. Louis, wrote Commissioner of Indian Affairs Hartly Crawford crowing, "Billy Caldwell's influence has been removed and the Potawatomi at Council Bluffs are now willing to draw a new treaty and remove to Kansas." Mitchell's glee was premature. Billy Caldwell was dead, but his influence was very much alive among the Prairie bands in Iowa. There his friends and clients, the Potawatomi wkamek, immediately set out to subvert the loyalties and to purchase the services of someone like Caldwell, seeking as his replacement a man with similar skills. And they also soon demonstrated they intended to honor his memory with a monument created after their fashion. Some months after his death they first proposed to American officials what they had in mind, while four years later-hard pressed to sign a new treaty-they countered with a long, detailed list of demands. At the top of this list was their tribute to Billy Caldwell: henceforth they wished to be officially identified as "The Prairie Indians of Caldwell's Band of Potowatomies." There was, these traditional leaders so indicated, a residue of supernormal power inherent in Caldwell's name, and, after their custom, they wished to preserve it.[75]

Born in a Mohawk village far to the east, Billy Caldwell lived his life in a succession of complex frontier communities, assuming such identities as were needed to give meaning to his living there, dreaming of what manner of man he might become, wondering about the judgements that would be formed of him after his leaving. When he died he was first laid in the soil nearby his home at Trader's Point. But as Council Bluffs grew his bones were reinterred in the Catholic cemetery, under a stone marked simply, "Indian." On the end, Billy Caldwell lay buried under the weight of an American racial stereotype.[76]

FOOTNOTES

1. This paper is an expanded version of a presentation for a symposium on Ethnogenesis on the Great lakes frontier during the annual meetings of the American Historical Association, 30 December 1976. It consists of a byproduct of a long term study of changing cultural adaptations of the Potawatomi, Odawa, Ojibwa, and wendat in Upper Canada and the Old Northwest. Original funded by the National Science Foundation and the Wenner-Gren Foundation, this research most recently has been supported by the National Museum of Man, Ottawa. Assistance received from these sources is gratefully acknowledged.
2. A discussion of the distinction between segmentary tribes (e.g., the Potawatomi) and chiefdoms (e.g., the Miami) will be found in Sahlins 1968: 14-27.
3. Bennett 1976: 10-11
4. See Sturtevant 1971 for a discussion of ethnogenesis.
5. Tanner 1976, and Peterson 1976.
6. For Billy's use of this title see any of his official correspondence in the period 1813-1819, in RG10 and MG24-B147, much of which is cited hereafter. He continued to use this title in his later years. See his letter printed in the *Chicago Daily Tribune*, 9 June 1840, reprinted in Wentworth 1912: 60.
7. Potawatomi leadership roles are fully discussed in Clifton 1975 and 1977.
8. See Paine 1971: 4-7 for technical definitions of the various middleman roles discussed in this essay.
9. For documentation of Billy's appointment, see Alexander Robinson's statement in DRC 21S: 282-83; Grover 1915: 98-99; Robertson and Riker I: 6-8, and 792-93; and Haydon 1934: 242-53. Conway's treatment of this matter is larded with ethnocentric errors (1975). In particular, Shawanese ("Little Changing Rain") is a personal name for a different man; it is not the same name or person as Sakonosh ("The Anglo-Canadian") which the Potawatomi sometimes used in referring to Billy Caldwell, and which Americans mistakenly assumed was a personal name. It was Shawanense, not Sakonosh that was written on the 1829 treaty at Prairie du Chien. Billy Caldwell's appellation, Sakonosh, appears only on the 1833 Treaty of Chicago.
10. See Margary 1878 I: 551-85, and 629-35; also Clifton 1977: 00-00.
11. For the source of Caldwell's given name, see his half brother, William Caldwell, Jr's., statement in DRC 17S229-235. For examples of Potawatomi leaders use of the name Billy Caldwell, see Abtekzhek ("Half Day's") speech, 27 Sept. 1839, in DIBIO 2: 4; T.R. Harvey's Minutes of a Council at Council Bluffs, 23 June 1845, in NAM 235, R 216; and Captain John Gantt's Report of Treaty Negotiations, Aug.-Sept., 1839 in NAM 234, R 215.

12. Scull 1967: 148

13. The first appearance of this phrase was in 1775. See "half-breed," Oxford Unabridged Dictionary. For a sterling analysis of the use of this category and the status of "half-breeds" farther west, see Brown 1975.

14. Casselman 1902: 139-40. In f.n.1, p. 139, Richardson's editor, Casselman, mistakenly identifies "Mr. William Caldwell" as Billy's father, Captain (later, Colonel) William Caldwell, Sr. It was Billy Caldwell, not his father, whose wounding at the Raisin River fought was described by Major Richardson. Care must be exercised in not confusing all the separate William Caldwells or Billy Caldwells of Upper Canada in this period as one and the same person. These included Billy himself, his father, William, Sr., and his half-brother, William Jr. A fourth William Caldwell-a client to John Askin, Jr., lived on the Upper Thames River in these same years, while a fifth William Caldwell received a land grant and settled on the Grand River. Whether the William Caldwell sometimes mentioned in Tipton papers as bidding on contracts in Indiana Territory is any one of these five men or a sixth different person is impossible to determine from available documents. Similarly, a "Chief Caldwell" led a small group of Ojibwa at Point Pelee in these years, for which see Clifton 1975, but he was apparently no relation to the other Caldwells mentioned.

15. Here I employ the standard anthropological distinction between emic (folk) and etic (analytic) categories. For a good discussion of various folk models of social race, see Wagley 1968 and Harris 1968 and 1971.

16. For examples of the use and application of the category of "half-breed" during Billy Caldwell's own lifetime, involving himself and persons known and important to him, see Francis Bond Head to Lord Glenelg, 4 April 1837, in MG11, Q Series, V. 396, part 4; Anthony Wayne to Major General H. Knox, 12 November 1794, in Knopf 1960: 362; Klinck and Talman 1970: 186; Proceedings of Council at Amherstburg, 31 August 1819, in RG 10, V. 489: 29540-52; William Claus to Captain Loring, 9 May 1814, in RG 10, V. 3: 75769. In general, none of these applications or characterizations of the "half-breed" stressed putatively innate, biological causes. rather, they emphasized behavioral traits, learned and perhaps malleable. The best study of variation in the use and growth in popularity of this category is in Brown 1975. What the Prairie Potawatomi thought of "half-breeds" (they stressed disloyalty) and how they treated them is discussed in Clifton 1977: 000-00. For a prime example of their thinking, see old Padegoshek (Pile of Lead's") Message to the Great White-Father, 27 July 1842 in NAM 234, R 215. It is noteworthy that the Potawatomi did not classify Billy Caldwell as a "Half-breed," and that numerous Americans continued to classify him as a (suspect) Englishman. See, particularly, Sub-Agent John Dougherty to SIA G. McGurie, 29 Jan. 1839, in NAM 234, R 215.

17. Standard treatments of Billy Caldwell's life are found in DAB 16: 376-77; Hodge 1911 1" 408; Burley 1919; Robertson and Riker 1942 1: 792-93; Brown 1944: 304-10; and the Billy Caldwell entries found in DIBIO. All of these are based on earlier, secondary versions of Billy's

life, especially Matson 1876 and 1880; Andreas 1884 1: 125; Hickling and Hubbard 1887; Kinzie 1857: 144-45; 186-87. 204, 239, and 253; Fulton 1882: 166; and Wentworth 1912. Noteworthy is the fact that all such versions, and Conway's later (1973) attempt, ignore the critically important interviews Lyman Draper obtained from Billy's own brothers and other contemporaries, including William, Jr. and James Caldwell, Alexander Robinson, and Mark Beaubien, for which see, DRC 21S274, 21S282-88, 17S238-40, and 17S229-35. Important manuscript collections are in CHS; MHS; RG 10, especially Vols. 4, 28, 30-34; PAC, the Caldwell Files, FMNHP; and MG 24, B147 (for which see PAC Finding Aid no. 845).

18. Kinzie 1857: 186-87.

19. Conway 1972 and 1975. This author is very confused about Potawatomi customs and institutions.

20. See Windsor Star, 11 and 12 Dec. 1973 and 21 Jan. 1974; London Free Press, 29 Oct. 1973 and 22 Feb. 1974; Toronto Globe and Mail, 19 Feb. 1974; and Chatham Daily News, 21 Jan. 1974. These developments are discussed and interpreted in Clifton 1975b: 110-117.

21. Caldwell's will is in Ontario 1-718, Will no. 199; it was probated 1822, Surrogate Court, Essex County, Windsor, Non Contentious Business Book No. 271-70. Both are in GS-OA.

22. B. Caldwell to F. Caldwell, 17 March 1834 in CHS.

23. DRC 17S238, and 17S229.

24. The document is in MG 21 Vol. B 225, Pt. 1: 185. I am indebted to Professor Clifford Abbott for his efforts at translations of this piece. Biographical sketches of Daniel Claus and William Claus are in Allen 1976: 106-109.

25. William Caldwell's career is briefly summarized in Allen 1976: 107. See Caldwell's own autobiographical sketch in his Draft of a Memorial to the Government, 1815, in OA, 20-135: 26, as well as the statement of his sons William and James cited above, f.n. 11. His commission in Butler's Rangers is located in RCA 1886: 640 or MG 21, B85, Pt. 1: 69. Instructions to and reports from and about his military activities are scattered through numerous sources, especially RCA 1882, Vols. 1 & 2, and 1883-1886; MG 19, A1, Vol. 3; MG 21, B21 (microfilm A687); and MG 21, B104 (21764), B101-102, B121, and B123. Of course he walks through the pages of numerous histories of the Revolutionary War, the Old Northwest, and Upper Canada. See especially Greymount 1972 (for his work with Butler's Ranger's), Horseman 1964 (for his post-war association with Matthew Elliot), and LaJuenesse 1960 (for his later career in Amherstburg).

26. To be fully accurate, Billy had no Potawatomi genitrix, although he may have acquired a mater from that tribe by informal adoption in his later years. Similarly, William Caldwell was Billy's genitor, but it was Daniel and William Claus who served him as socially responsible pater.

27. F. Haldimand to Brig. Gen. Powell, 21 April 1782, in MG21, B104 (21764): 270-71. See Caldwell's own report of the Upper Sandusky fight,

as well as that of his Lieutenant, John Turney, in Caldwell to DePeyster, 11 June 1782, MG 21, B102: 65-66; and Turney to DePeyster, 7 June 1782, in RCA 1887: 237. Horseman (1964: 36-39) summarized the sense and details of this engagement nicely.

28. See Klinck and Talman 1970: xvii-lxxxix; and Johnston 1964.

29. See DRC 17S238-39 and 17S229-30. The name of Billy's mother is unknown; however her father was the Mohawk leader The Rising Son.

30. Erikson 1975: 269-71.

31. DRC 17S230-231 and 17S239-40; Prideaux Selby to Col. Alexander McKee, 9 May 1973, in Cruikshank 1931 5:40. For examples of this sort of linguistic interference in Captain Billy's writing, see his letters to William Claus, 27 April 1816, in MG 24, B 147: 48-51; and to Duncan Cameron, 28 August 1815, in RG 10, V. 31: 18369-71.

32. For documentation of the basic facts concerning his career in this period see Alexander Robinson's statement, DRC 21S282-88 Robert Forsyth's statement, DRC 22S105-106; and William and James Caldwell's statements, DRC 17S230-31 and 239-40.

33. For details of Captain Billy's marriages and children, see DRC 21S284 and 17S229-35; also Caldwell family genealogy in FMNHP. Neskotnemek is generally translated as "Mad Sturgeon"; however, it translates more accurately as "Angry man of the Fish (Totem)." He and his brother Wabinema were important leaders of the Sturgeon lineage of the Fish clan in these years.

34. B. Caldwell to F. Caldwell, 17 April 1834, in Caldwell Papers, CHS.

35. Quaife 1913: 148-50; Robinson statement, DRC 21S282-84; William Caldwell, Jr., statement, DRC 17S231-32; Billy Caldwell to William Claus, 27 April 1816, MG 24 B147: 49-51.

36. Tucker 1956: 258; Drake 1858: Ch. 18.

37. B. Caldwell to W. Claus, 27 April 1816, MG 24, B147: 49.

38. See Durfee 1970; Caldwell to Claus, 27 April 1816, MG 24, B147: 50; Kinzie Forsyth Ledger Book A: 60, in MHS; Caldwell to Cameron, 28 August 1815, in RG 10, V. 31: 18369-71 (in this letter Billy actually wrote, while very drunk and depressed, "I have not mist (sic) a Battle since January, 1812-which (when) I had the honor of cooperating with the Right Division." The reference clearly is to the River Raisin fight, 22 January 1813, and in his stupor Billy misplaced a year); Wentworth 1912: 62-63; Clarke 1870: 114-15; and Tucker 1956: 314.

39. Kinzie 1856; DRC 21S283 and 17S232; and Williams 1953. In mid-May, 1812, Matthew Irwing, U.S. Factor at Chicago, reported that a "Caldwell" residing in Amherstburg had been seen on the St. Joseph River heading for the Shawnee Prophet's camp (Cater 1934: 16:221). This was not likely Billy Caldwell, who must have been known to Irwing as a resident of the Chicago area and an associate of the Kinzies and Forsyths. More likely, it was one of Billy's brothers, all of whom then lived in Amherstburg and who were serving their father's political, military, and economic interests.

40. Canadian archive sources contain no reference to or mention of Billy's

wife and children for the years 1813-1819, although at least one child, the ill-fated son Alexander, was born about 1814. For some details of Caldwell's Rangers, see Irving 1908: 95, 210, and 213; Proctor to Major Gen. Sheaffe, 13 Jan. 1813, in MG11, C Series, V. 678: 27; and William Caldwell, et al., 40 cont. Memorial to George Prevost, 26 Feb. 1813, in Farney, n.d. The exact date of Billy's commission in the Indian Department is unknown, but it could not have been much before January, 1813, when he is first reported on active service. Note that the "Captain Caldwell" noted by Major John Richardson as involved in the Fort Wayne campaign in September, 1812 was a militia officer. Hence this could not have been William Caldwell, Sr., William Caldwell, Jr., or Thomas Caldwell. See Casselman 1902: 296-300.

41. See Caton 1876: 17-18; Casselman 1902: 139; Tucker 1956: 314-17; Clarke 1870: 114-15; Irving 1908: 210; B. Caldwell's Certificate of Loss of Baggage, 5 Dec. 1815, in MG 11, C Series, V. 84; Major Glegg to Col. William Caldwell, 16 June, 1814, in RG 10, V. 3: 1408; Lt. Col. Drummond to Sir George Prevost, 7 July 1814, in MG 11, C Series, Vol. 684; and Major Glegg to Major Givens, 10 May 1814, RG 10, V. 34.

42. For background and many details, see Horseman 1964: 119-139 & 218-219; Allen 1976: 63-67; and Klinck and Talman 1970: cv-cxv; Billy Caldwell to William Caldwell, 8 Sept. 1814, in RG 10, V. 29; and B. Caldwell to Duncan Cameron, 11 May 1815, in RG 10, V. 30: 17959.

43. Return of Indians under Captains Billy Caldwell and Wilson, 7 June 1814, RG 10, V. 8; Captain Kerr to William Claus, 28 April 1814, RG 10, V. 3; B. Caldwell to Claus, 6 May 1814, RG 10, V. 28; Sir John Johnston to Lt. Col. Wm. Caldwell, 18 May 1814, in Caldwell Papers, FMNHP; Sir John Prevost to Lt. Gen. Drummond and Noah Freer (Military Secretary) to William Caldwell, 23 May 1814, RG 10, V. 3 `368-72; Anon (probably Matthew Elliot, Jr.), Complaints about Colonel Caldwell, 18 Dec. 1814, in RG 10, V. 29: 17494-500; and B. Caldwell to Anon., 6 May 1814, RG 10, V. 28.

44. Col. Caldwell to Col. Foster, Return of western Indians, 10 Oct. 1814, RG 10, V. 3: 1523-28; Proceedings of Council, 20 and 26 May 1814, RG 10, V. 3; Wm. Claus to Capt. Loring, 1 June 1814, RG 10, V. 3; B. Caldwell to Col. Caldwell, 8 Sept. 1814, RG 10, V. 29; Shawnee King (i.e., the Prophet. Tenskatawa) to Col. Caldwell, 21 Nov. 1814, RG 10, V. 3: 16-17; Col. Caldwell to Lt. Col. R. James, 1 Dec. 1814, in Wood 1968 3: 733-34; and Noah Freer to Gen. Drummond, 26 Jan. 1815, in MG 11, C Series, V. 1226, Pt. 2: 17-18.

45. MG 11, C Series, V. 167: 22; Andrew Cochrane (acting Deputy Judge Advocate) to Billy Caldwell, 10 Nov. 1814, in Caldwell Papers, FMNHP: 42.3.24.12; Gen. Proctor to B. Caldwell, 1 March 1815 in MG 24, B 147, 19-21; and Return of the Western Branch, 26 Jan. 1815, RG 10, V. 257: 376; Lt. Col. James to Harvey, 3 Dec. 1814, in Wood 1968 3: 733-34; and Noah Freer to Gen. Drummond, 26 Jan. 1815, in MG 11, C Series, V. 1226, Pt. 2: 17-18.

46. B. Caldwell to D. Cameron, 8 and 11 May 1815, RG 10 V. 30: 17940

and 17959; Wm. Claus to Lt. Co;. Foster, 22 May 1815, MG 11, C Series, V. 258: 78-79; Extract from General Orders No. 1, Quebec, 11 July 1815, MG 11, C Series, V. 258; Lt. Col. James to Maj. Gen. F.P. Robinson, 15 July 1815, MG 11, C Series, V. 258: 161-76.

47. For examples of Captain Billy's duties and his relations with his father in this period, see ZB. Caldwell to Gabriel Godfrey (U.S. Indian Agent, Detroit), 1 July 1815, V. 34: 19185-86; Godfrey to B. Caldwell, 5 July 1815, V. 34: 19189-91; B. Caldwell to D. Cameron, 10 August 1815 and 13 October 1815, V. 31: 18298-300 and 18519-20; and B. Caldwell to Wm. Claus, 27 April 1815, V. 30: 17843-44; all in RG 10.

48. For background on this period in Amherstburg and Fort Malden, see Allen 1976: 86-93. See also Lt. Col. James to Maj. Gen. F.P. Robinson, 15 July 1815, MG 11, C Series, V. 258: 161-71 and 16 July 1815, RG 10, V. 31: 18182-94.

49. Lt. Col. James to Sir Frederick Robinson, 15 July 1815, MG 11, C Series, V. 258: 161-67; James to Wm. Caldwell, Sr., 18 July 1815, MG 11, C Series,V. 258: 73; Robinson to Sir Gordon Drummond, 8 August 1815, RG 10, V. 31: 18173-75.

50. B. Caldwell to D. Cameron, 28 August 1815, V. 31: 18369-7. See also B. Caldwell to Wm. Claus, 2 Sept. 1815, V. 31 18438-40; both in RG 10. The third man Billy trusted with his private sentiments was his good friend and companion, Captain John Wilson.

51. Lt. Col. R. James, Amherstburg District Order, 21 Oct. 1815, MG 11, C Series, V. 258: 477. B. Caldwell to James, 22 Oct. 1815, RG 10, V. 4: 1820-21; Caldwell to D. Cameron, 22 Oct. 1815, RG 10, V. 4: 1825-26. See also Billy's accompanying letter to Wm. Claus that same date, in RG 10 V. 4: 1823-24; and James to B. Caldwell, 22 Oct. 1815, MG 11, C Series, V. 258: 479.

52. For examples of Billy's duties in the winter of 1815-1816 and the Spring and Summer of 1816, see Caldwell to Claus, 27 Mar. 1816, V. 32: 18956-58; to Claus, 1 July 1816, V. 33: 19184; and to Gabriel Godfrey, 1 July 1816, V. 34: 19185-86; all in RG 10. Bill's extensive correspondence in this period is continued in V. 34 of the same series.

53. Claus to B. Caldwell, 10 Nov. 1815, 40-41; and D. Cameron to B. Caldwell, 44-47; both in NG 24, B 147.

54. Wm. Claus to Sir Francis Gore, 22 Feb. 1816, RG 10, V. 4: 1927-38; John Askin Jr., to Claus, 5 March 1816, RG 10 V. 32: 18911-12; D. Cameron to B. Caldwell, 2 April 1816, RG 10, V. 34: 19296-97.

55. Claus to B. Caldwell, 12 April 1816, 55-56; *D. Cameron to B. Caldwell*, 13 April 1816, 57-58; Claus to Caldwell, 26 July 1816, 64-67; all in MG 24, B 147; also B. Caldwell to Claus, 12 Aug. 1816, RG 10, V. 34: 19296-97.

56. B. Caldwell to Wm. Claus, 27 April 1816, MG 24, B 147: 48-51.

57. Chamblee's Pass. 1 August 1816, in Billy Caldwell Papers, CHS; for Billy's other efforts at bestowing patronage in this period, see his extensive correspondence in MG 24, B 147 and RG 10, V. 32 and 34. Shabni is a morphonemic spelling of the name that generally appears as

Shabbona or Shobnee in American documents, which are usually mistranslated as "Bear Shoulders" or "Shaped Like a Bear."
58. General Orders, Headquarters, Quebec, 28 Dec. 1816, in RG 10, V. 33; General Orders, Establishment of the Indian Department, 27 Aug. 1816, MG 24, B 147: 72-72; B. Caldwell to Claus, 24 Sept. 1816, RG 10, V. 34: 19414-15.
59. John Wilson to B. Caldwell, 14 March 1817, 77-80; and Noah Freer to B. Caldwell, 22 July 1817, 86; both in MG 24.
60. Account of B. Caldwell with Berczy Macon & Co., 15 march 1817, MG 24, B 147: 81-82; Upper Canada Land Petitions C. Bundle 11, No. 183: 394, Billy Caldwell's Petition, York, 1 Sept. 1818; and Land Book J, Petitions Treated in Council, 5 Oct. 1818: 439; in Microfilms C-1652 and C-183, PAC.
61. Irving 1808: 210-212; Ontario 1-718, Will No. 199, William Caldwell, Sr.'s Last Will and Testament, Jan. 1818, in OA-GS; also, Inventory of Merchandise Remaining in Gosfield Concern, in MG 24, B 147: 94-97.
62. DRC 17S229-35.
63. DRC 21S284.
64. Kappler 1904: 145-55; For a more detailed study of developments in this period, including Billy Caldwell's involvement with the Potawatomi, see Clifton 1977; 000-00.
65. East 1944: 137.
66. Kappler 1904: 297-99; Hurlbutt 1881; Andreas 1884: 1: 91, 205, and 600.
67. B. Caldwell to Thomas Forsyth, 8 April 1832, in Tesson Collections, MHS.]
68. T. Forsyth to B. Caldwell, 10 Sept. 1832, in Forsyth papers, MHS. See also, R.A. Forsyth to T. Forsyth, 14 April 1833, Tesson Collections, MHS.
69. See Clifton 1977: 000-00 for a discussion of Caldwell's role at the 1833 treaty.
70. B. Caldwell to F. Caldwell, 17 March 1834, in Caldwell Papers, CHS. Also, B. Woodridge to Hon. Henry Clay, 16 Dec. 1833. Woodridge Papers, BHC.
71. K. Dougherty to G. McGuire, SIA, St. Louis, 29 Jan. 1839. Also Capt. John Gantt's Report of Treaty Negotiations. Aug. - Sept. 1839, in R. 215, NAM 234, and, DIBIO 2: 4.
72. Chittenden and Richardson 1905: 157 & 173; Van der Zee 1913: 3; Cummins 1933: 9-10; and Chicago Daily Tribune, 9 June 1840.
73. East 1944: 137; Report of Stephen Cooper, Sub-Agent, Council Bluffs, 2 Oct. 1841, DIBIO 2: 4' P. D. Clarke to Francis Caldwell, 15 Sept. 1843, in MG 24, B 147: 198-200.
74. Mitchell to Crawford, 29 Feb, 1842, R. 215, NAM 234.
75. T.H. Harvey's Minutes of Council at Council Bluffs, 23 June 1845, R 216, NAM 234.
76. Pruitt 1954.

ABBREVIATIONS USED IN NOTES

BHC BURTON HISTORICAL COOLLECTIONS, DETROIT PUBLIC LIBRARY.
CHS LIBRARY AND ARCHIVES, CHICAGO HISTORICAL SOCIETY, CHICAGO HISTORY MUSEUM.
DAB DUMAS MALONE, ED., DICTIONARY OF AMERICAN BIOGRAPHY, 20 VOLS., NEW YORK, SCRIBNERS.
DIBIO UNITED STATES DEPARTMENT OF THE INTERIOR, BIOGRAPHICAL AND HISTORICAL INDEX OF AMERICAN INDIANS AND PERSONS INVOLVED IN INDIAN AFFAIRS. 8 VOLS., BOSTON, G.K. HALL AND COMPANY, 1966.
DRC THE LYMAN DRAPER MANUSCRIPT COLLECTIONS. MADISON, STATE HISTORICAL COLLECTIONS OF WISCONSIN.
FMNHP ARCHIVES AND LIBRARY, FORT MALDEN NATIONAL HISTORICAL PARK. AMHERSTBURG, ONTARIO.
MG 11 C SERIES TRANSCRIPTS OF COLONIAL OFFICE RECORDS. OTTAWA, PUBLIC ARCHIVES OF CANADA.
MG 11 Q SERIES TRANSCRIPTS OF COLONIAL OFFICE PAPERS FROM THE PUBLIC RECORDS OFFICE, LONDON. PUBLIC ARCHIVES OF CANADA, OTTAWA.
MG 19 F1 CLAUS FAMILY PAPERS. OTTAWA, PUBLIC ARCHIVES OF CANADA.
MG 21 THE HALDIMAN COLLECTION. ADDITONAL MANUSCRIPTS 21661-21892. OTTAWA, PUBLIC ARCHIVES OF CANADA.
MG 24 B 147 CALDWELL FAMILY PAPERS, OTTAWA, PUBLIC ARCHIVES OF CANADA.
MHS ARCHIVES AND LIBRARY, MISSOURI HISTORICAL SOCIETY, ST. LOUIS.
NAM 234 NATIONAL ARCHIVES MICROCOPY 234. LETTER RECEIVED BY THE OFFICE OFINDIAN AFFAIRS. 962 MICROFILM ROLLS. WASHINGTOM, D.C., NATIONAL ARCHIVES AND RECORDS SERVICE.
QA-GS ONTARIO ARCHIVES-GENERAL SERIES. TORONTO, ONTARIO PROVINCIAL ARCHIVES.
QAR ALEXANDER FRASER, ED., REPORT OF THE BUREAU OF ARCHIVES FOR THE PROVINCE OF ONTARIO, TORONTO (CONTINUING SERIES, 1903-PRESENT).
PAC PUBLIC ARCHIVES OF CANADA.
RCA BRYMER, D., A.G. DOUGHERTY, AND G. LANCTOT, EDS. REPORT ON THE CANADIAN ARCHIVES (CONTINUING SERIES, 1872-PRESENT). OTTAWA, PUBLIC ARCHIVES OF CANADA.

CHAPTER 4

FOR HE WAS A BAD SON

For the story of the "Bad Son," I am indebted to the Reverend Lewis Pfaller, Professor of History at Assumption Abbey, Richardton, North Dakota. I am also indebted to the State Historical Society of North Dakota for permission to use the work in whole or in part for this book. It was originally published in North Dakota History (Vol. 36, No. 2, 1969, pp. 121 - 139), as "The Brave Bear Murder Case." The "Bad Son" is a man known in time as Mato Ohitika or Brave Bear. In his time he was probably better known by his nickname, Wapepe (Smart Character).[1]

As one reads the record of the misdeeds of this seemingly evil son, one must look closely at what may have impelled him to act as he did. It is a dangerous journey looking back in time and trying to reason out what this man was really like. Perhaps, the record should just speak for itself. Wapepe certainly can't do it anymore, and judgement is certainly reserved for a higher judge then me. However, one can certainly wonder what storms ran through the mind of such a person.

Read then, the story of a murderer, and a procurer of women for evil purposes.

Mato Ohitika (Brave Bear) from a Goff photgraph.
Courtesy: State Historical Society of North Dakota

SANTEE DAKOTA - CUT HEAD BAND, YANKTON (SIOUX)

"It is well," replied Red Shield. "We are glad, his mother and myself, for he was a bad son."[2] These were the words of a father; the father of a young man named Brave Bear, (1850?-1882). Red Shield had just learned that his son had perished at the end of the hangman's rope.

What had Brave Bear done that had led him to the hangman's rope? Let us go backwards into time and hear the story of a man who may have been simply the product of his times, or else, a man who was truly a miscreant. I have excerpted the story as researched, written and presented by the Reverend Louis Pfaller, O.S.B., and as it was published in North Dakota History in 1969. Numbering of footnotes varies from the original, as this author has added what thoughts and knowledge he has of Brave Bear and his times. Otherwise, the narrative is unchanged from the original.

"...Brave Bear was an Indian 'dude,' a sort of dandy with plenty of flashy clothes and cheap jewelry. The vain, cunning and unprincipled young Sioux attracted a handful of rowdies about him and made life miserable for the more peaceably inclined. At the time of his execution, it was stated that he had killed as many as thirty Indians, although this was probably an exaggeration. We can only recount here several of the exploits that are certain.

The first 'shocker' we know of occurred on July 5, 1874, when he and his little gang brutally slew three Chippewa metis near Walhalla, then known as St. Joe, along the Pembina River in Dakota. In searching for a motive for the triple murder of the innocent half-breeds, we find the best explanation in the testimony of an Indian scout, Hupshanskaska, who met the murderers soon after the ghastly deed.[3] They told the scout that, in a recent scrape with the Rees, (note * in the original text with identification of 'Rees,' as Arickara) the other Yanktonnais reproached the Cut Heads with cowardice, and that they determined to kill some Chippewas to prove the contrary.

Brave Bear's gang consisted of Ish-naki-yapi (The Only One), He-ha-ha-ton-ka (Night Owl, or Big Voice in the Night), and Sunk-sa-pa (Black Horse). They had been hunting with a caravan of some fifty seven lodges of Cut Heads, and had arrived on the Devils lake Reservation on June 27, 1874, to visit some of their relatives near Fort Totten. When the agency farmer, George Faribault, asked them why they were not living on the Standing Rock Reservation, Brave Bear invented the story that the principal men of the Devils Lake Agency were going to Washington to visit the Great Father, and that he wanted to join them.[4]

A few days later, Brave Bear came to agency headquarters for more guest provisions and also asked for powder and lead. Faribault gave them food but no ammunition, and the band set out toward Standing Rock. Soon the four renegades slipped away from the other Cut Heads and proceeded towards the northeast. Toward the east end of Devils lake the malevolent gang camped near the home of an Indian named Tomacheha. Brave Bear's brother-in-law, less wicked than the rest, came to the house under the pretense of asking for matches and warned the Indian not to leave his family and property. He said that Brave Bear disliked the conduct of the Fort Totten Indians in building houses and in living in harmony with the Chippewas, the Gros Ventres, the Mandan and the Rees, and that he wanted to break it up: that they were determined to kill some Chippewas for this purpose.[5]

A few days later, the four came to the Chippewa settlements near present Walhalla, North Dakota. One account says that Brave Bear did not attack the first Chippewa he met. He was looking for a certain Langis (maybe Langie or Longie) who had done them a bad turn during a trip into the Sioux country. By chance the very first man they met was Langis, but they did not recognize him. Langis suspected their intentions, and when asked where he lived, Langis pointed to the home of Joseph De Lorme.[6]

Living with De Lorme was his wife, Isabelle, his son, Louis, his daughter, Nancy, Baptiste Moran, Nancy's husband, and seven children. It was noon of July 5, when the vengeful band rode up to the De Lorme dwelling. What happened next is told in various forms in the several accounts, but the one that seems most reliable is that given by Captain J. S. Naught of Fort Pembina, who visited the place soon after and reported on July 8,

'Upon entering the house, they stood their guns against the wall. The occupants of the house offered to shake hands with the Indians. The Indians declined. The occupants then asked them to eat, and Mrs. De Lorme went to the kitchen to bring food. When she put it on the table, the Indians took their guns and left the house. The occupants followed them out, and as they went, were met by the Indians, who commenced firing, killing two men - Louie De Lorme and Baptiste Moran - instantly, mortally wounding a third - Joseph De Lorme who died about 4 P.M. same day, and slightly wounded the woman - Mrs. Joseph De Lorme - flesh wound in the finger. In addition to the flesh wound Mrs. De Lorme received other injuries, the results of kicking and beating inflicted upon her by the Indians. One other woman - Mrs. Moran - was knocked down with the butt of a gun, and received several scalp wounds. A young man, Bernal De Lorme, escaped through a window, when the firing commenced. The other occupants of the house (all children) made good their escape. Mrs. Moran started for the woods, where she remained until 10 o'clock next morning when she was found in a very weak condition, and suffering from her wounds, by some half-breeds who had gone out to search for her. In addition to the gunshot wounds, Joseph and Louis De Lorme each received sabre wounds, the former over the right side of the head, and on the arms and hands, and the latter in the chest.'[7]

According to Mrs. De Lorme's grandson, her life was spared when the shot at close range lodged in the metal crucifix she was wearing. The impact had stunned her, and she was left for dead.[8]

The murderers calmly went to the stable and took six horses before fleeing southwest. On the way, several of the horses played out and were left behind. When they camped next day at Lake Belland (now called Lake Juanita in Foster County) on the Fort Seward-Fort Totten Trail, they tried to trade horses with some freighters who were camped there.

The fleeing Indians arrived in Jamestown early on July 7, boasting that they had killed some Chippewas up north and displayed one fresh scalp, according to scout Henry Belland. The scout later testified: 'I visited the camp of the Indians near Fort Seward, and found the party to consist of four men who had eight horses in their possession. The four Indians were in war costume and had their faces blackened, which is a sign that they had killed an enemy.[9] The scout with Belland recognized the De Lorme horses, and this evidence, together with the sword Belland found on the Indians' trail north of Jamestown on July 8, pointed quite definitely to this band as the guilty ones when the news became general.

From Jamestown the Indians fled west of the Missouri,

where they fritted about the Yantonnais camps along the Cannonball and Missouri Rivers. That fall, Deputy U.S. Marshal Edgerly sought to get troops to help him arrest several murderers on Standing Rock Reservation, including Rain in the Face and The Man That Buggers. On November 24, the marshal returned without the murderers, because Agent Edmund Palmer declined to help for fear of stirring up his Indians.[10]

Soon afterwards, General George A. Custer at Fort Abraham Lincoln sent Captain George W. Yates with two companies of the Seventh Cavalry, guided by Lonesome Charley Reynolds, to the agency to arrest Rain in the Face, who had killed two men on Custer's expedition along the Yellowstone in the summer of 1873. In order to throw Rain in the Face off his guard, Yates announced that he was looking for the murderers of the De Lormes. When Rain in the Face confidently entered the trader's store on issue day, the troops seized him. The Indians were greatly excited, and their anger at the presence of the troops produced an unexpected dividend. Custer tells the story in a telegram to Departmental Headquarters in St. Paul, dated December 24, 1874:

'Immediately after the arrest of Rain in the Face, I notified a party of Indians who had accompanied him to this post that there were other murderers at the agency who might expect to be arrested. This remark was conveyed to the tribe, and through fear of a second visit from the troops, the chiefs of Two Bear's band forced Brave Bear, a young Yanktonnais warrior, to set out alone with the purpose of delivering himself up at this post. He was met this side of the agency by an officer of the civil law. Today he arrived at this post and is now confined in the guard house. He confessed to me today voluntarily that he and three others murdered a white man on the Red River some months ago. His three companions fled a few days ago to Cheyenne Agency. Their names are known.'[11]

Just how long he was detained at Fort Abraham Lincoln is not certain. The date of Custer's next communication is March 8, 1876, though it seems more likely that it was 1875. Whichever it was, Custer wrote to Agent Palmer:

'A few days ago I had occasion to write to you concerning the health of Brave Bear, confined at this post by the civil authorities. He was placed in the hospital and received all the care and attention his situation demanded. Last night between the hours of 9 and 12 o'clock Brave Bear made his escape from the hospital taking with him property of the U.S., consisting of three (3) hospital blankets, one pair of slippers, and one pair of overshoes belonging to a private party. I have ordered the country below this post to be scouted in search of Brave Bear. The Commanding Officer at Fort Rice has also been requested to send parties out between his post and Standing Rock. I presume, however, that Brave Bear will be enabled to reach the village to which he belongs. I write to inform you of the facts and to request you to make a demand upon his tribe for his surrender to military authorities. Please inform them that if this demand is not complied with, cavalry will be sent to make a thorough search of every lodge at the agency. Brave Bear has already had a preliminary examination before the U.S. Commissioner at Bismarck upon the charge upon which he was arrested, and was committed for trial at the next term of court. If his band will comply promptly with the above demand, they will save themselves much trouble and annoyance.'[12]

Palmer promptly replied that Brave Bear was on the east side of the Missouri, near the agency, quite sick and doctored by the Indians. They refused to give him up, but would not resist if troops were sent. A detachment sallied forth from Fort Rice to nab him, but he vanished before they arrived.

It seems that he returned when the danger had passed, and lived in the Yantonnais camps, succeeding even in being designated as one of the chiefs. He acquired a taste for liquor, and in order to get money to but the fire-water, made a business of securing Indian women as prostitutes for the whites at Fort Yates. Agent Hughes thereupon determined to depose him from his chieftanship.[13] Things were getting hot for Brave Bear, and lest he should be arrested again, he decided to move to the Cut Head camp at Devils Lake.

It was November, 1877, when Brave Bear and his father, Wahacankaduta (Red Shield), arrived at McLaughlin's agency to live with his relatives. Red Shield was a good, quiet Indian, but his son and The Only One soon made it very disagreeable for the other Indians, and numerous complaints were lodged against them.[14] McLaughlin viewed this as open defiance of law and order, and determined to arrest the murderers.

In February, 1878, McLaughlin wrote to Thomas Van Etten, U.S. Commissioner in Bismarck, to obtain a warrant to arrest the troublesome pair. Van Etten replied on March 2, 'These Indians should be arrested and confined at Totten till the Marshal gets there for them. If you arrest or cause them to be arrested, the marshall will start as soon as I am informed of their apprehension. It was a damnable murder and they should be punished. If they are arrested, have them shackled so they can't jump the guard, as was the case before.'15

Captain James M. Bell of Fort Totten put nine soldiers at McLaughlin's disposal, and the agent planned to make a swift move to capture them at the Cut Head camp at Crow Hill, but George Faribault advised against it because of the danger of a fight and escape. McLaughlin resorted instead to set a clever trap. He called a council of all the adult members of the Cut Heads on the second floor of the main agency building, under the pretense of ascertaining the acreage each family intended to cultivate that year, so as to determine the amount of seed to be ordered.16

On the appointed day, March 16, Lt. Herbert J. Slocum waited at nearby Fort Totten with his eight men, to come on the double on a pre-arranged signal. Brave Bear and The Only One were the last to arrive and as soon as they were in the room the soldiers rushed up the stairs. The doors and windows were guarded by agency employees and the murderers were trapped. The assembled Indians were tremendously excited, but McLaughlin soon quieted them by announcing that only the criminals would be arrested.

As the soldiers were descending the stairs, Brave Bear sprained his ankle and put up no resistance, but The Only One gave a mighty leap, knocking down the soldier ahead, and then he bounded over him and rounded the corner of the building. He ran in a wild zig-zag pattern, as bullets whistled round him. When no one seemed to be able to hit him, an old grizzled sergeant dropped on one knee, took careful aim, and sent a ball into the speedster's leg. Screaming in pain and frustration, The Only One drew his knife and charged at the soldiers. The sergeant shot again, sending a fatal shot into the heart of the slayer.

Brave Bear was confined in the Fort Totten guardhouse, making it necessary to crowd the military prisoners into one small room. After a month of waiting for the U.S. Deputy Marshal to come from Bismarck, Captain Bell wrote to Attorney Van Etten at Bismarck that if the Marshal did not come soon, he would like to set Brave Bear free. McLaughlin wrote too, pleading the cause of Captain Bell. It was not his fault, replied Van Etten, on April 23. He had delivered the warrant to Ben Ash, the Deputy U.S. Marshal, but Ash was delayed by lack of funds. He regretted the inconvenience Brave Bear was causing Fort Totten, but pleaded, 'Don't let him go as there is evidence enough to hang him.'[17]

Ben Ash finally came to take the prisoner some time in May. On the way from Fort Totten to Bismarck, they became quite friendly and Brave Bear acknowledged his part in the crime. Ash, however, took no chances with him and handcuffed his prisoner to his left wrist each night before going to sleep.

In Bismarck he was lodged in a log jail awaiting transfer to Fargo for trial. Ash recalled years later that each day as he passed the jail, the Indian was always standing on a chair, looking through the bars. 'Ben! Ben! Tobac', tobac',' was his daily salutation, and the deputy marshal kept him supplied with tobacco.[18]

The trial was set to take place in Fargo in early August, and preparations were begun. When Brave Bear asked George P. Flannery of Bismarck to be his attorney, he offered his horses as fees. Flannery then wrote to McLaughlin to verify the defendant's claims to wealth, and on June 29 the agent replied: '...I have seen the father of Wapepe who says that he has two ponies and his sister has an American horse and he has other friends who have several ponies and they are willing to give them all as soon as they see his son set free.

It is difficult to make an Indian understand this kind of business litigation. They think that by paying a set amount any guilty man can, and should be given his liberty.'[19]

It seems that Flannery would not defend Brave Bear under these conditions, especially since the evidence for conviction was so overwhelming. The testimony of Mrs. De Lorme and Mrs. Moran who had witnessed the murders, and the testimony of Henry Belland, who still had the blood-stained sabre, would be too much to overthrow. A speedy conviction seemed in the making as the court convened in Fargo on August 5, 1878. Speedy it was, but the verdict shocked and chagrined McLaughlin, who was present.

Attorneys S. G. Comstock of Moorhead and A. B. Guptill of Fargo had apparently been appointed by the court to defend the Indian, and they found a loophole which compelled Judge A. H. Barnes to dismiss the case. They claimed, first, that the offense had been committed in the Pembina district, and that the Fargo district lacked jurisdiction; secondly, they charged that two of the grand jurors who indicted Brave Bear were not qualified to act as jurors.

Judge Barnes therefore issued an order remanding Brave Bear to the custody of the U.S. Marshal, J. B. Raymond, that the slayer might be tried at Pembina when the court should convene there. What happened at Pembina, McLaughlin relates in his book, *My Friend the Indian:*

He was put in jail at Pembina, and one morning he was missing. With him went the horse of the jailor [George Parker]. Brave Bear declared afterwards that his medicine was good and had liberated him; that he had simply invoked the power of his medicine and floated through the roof of the jail. As to the disappearance of the jailor's horse, why that might have been a part of the medicine.20

He rode quickly to the Devils Lake Reservation, where he arrived on the evening of October 3 at the home of his father, Red Shield, and his brother, Elk. Fearing arrest, he set out after a few hours, accompanied by his relatives.21 The latter settled once more on Standing Rock and were as peaceful as they had been on the Devils Lake Reservation, but Brave Bear sought refuge on the Pine Ridge Reservation.

He soon found himself in ill favor at Pine Ridge, and he then fled to the Crow Creek Reservation, below present Pierre, South Dakota. Accounts of what happened next vary in details, but the version given by Ben Ash seems quite accurate.22 In he middle of May, 1879, Brave Bear learned that a man named Agar (maybe Agard) was going to drive to Standing Rock, and he begged to ride along. On May 15, about sundown, they arrived at a point where the trail branched off to old Fort Sully. As Agar turned his team into the side trail, Brave Bear asked where he was going. 'Down to Fort Sully to spend the night,' Agar replied. 'Wait,' the Indian exclaimed as he climbed out of the rig, 'I don't go down there where they have all those soldiers. I'll walk on up the trail a ways and sleep out tonight. I'll get in the wagon when you overtake me tomorrow,'

Agar resumed his journey the next morning and drove on to Standing Rock without seeing his traveling companion again. Although he knew of Brave Bear's treachery, he thought little about the affair at the time.

After leaving Agar the previous evening, Brave Bear had walked on to the Okobojo Creek, at a point some twenty miles from Fort Sully. He lay down in the tall grass to sleep and was awakened by the approach of a traveler named Joseph Johnson, a hard-working man who had saved up $1,700 and was now riding from Fort Sully to the James River country. He hoped to meet his brother near present Redfield, South Dakota, where they planned to take up land and establish a cattle ranch.

Instead of making his presence known, Brave Bear dropped down again and remained silent while the ex-soldier picketed his horse, prepared a meal over a camp fire and then went to sleep for the night. Then Brave Bear murdered the sleeping man, stripped his body and put on his clothes with the $1,700 in bills. Mounting Johnson's horse he rode on to Standing Rock, arriving there in advance of Agar, but keeping out of sight until Agar had attended to his business and returned to Crow Agency.

The people of Standing Rock, well acquainted with Brave Bear's character, became suspicious of his sudden prosperity. 'The Injun's done something again,' remarked scout E.H. "Fish" Allison, but before the news of the murder caught up, Brave Bear was on the trail. A few days later, about the end of May, he arrived on the Devils lake Reservation, and sought out his uncle, whom he persuaded to go to the trading post and buy him forty dollars worth of provisions. He tried to keep hidden, but almost immediately he was recognized by the wife of one of the Indian policemen, and she hastened to tell her husband. The policeman at once procured reenforcements and proceeded to arrest Brave Bear. The uncle quickly alerted Brave Bear, and the wily criminal thought up a cunning ruse to give himself time to escape. He spread the rumor that 3,000 hostile Sioux were on their way to kill everybody at the agency and that he had gone to warn his uncle. In the fear and confusion that followed, he made good his escape, and joined the hostile Sioux under Sitting Bull in Canada.[23]

Mrs. F. C. Holley, who worked for a number of years on the Standing Rock Reservation and knew George Faribault well, relates that when Brave Bear reached Sitting Bull's camp he plotted further mischief:

'...he tried to get a half-dozen Indians there to join him, and start back on the war-path, for the purpose of killing Major McLaughlin and Mr. Faribault, as they had been the cause of his arrest. His plan of operation was, on reaching the Agency, to call in the night at the house of Mr. Faribault, who would be the person to open the door, when directly upon his appearance he would shoot him. From there he would go directly to Major McLaughlin's, rap at the door and greet him in the same manner. Brave Bear failed to raise the followers which he needed, and without a force to support him, his scheme for slaughter and revenge was again a failure.'24

In the meantime, searchers found the body of Joseph Johnson near Okobojo Creek, and the evidence pointed strongly toward Brave Bear. Since Johnson had been a member of the Odd Fellows, they offered a sizeable reward for the capture of Brave Bear. Then in 1880-1881, Fish Allison, who had seen Brave Bear with Johnson's horse and rifle soon after the murder, was employed as a scout and messenger to induce the fugitive Sioux under Sitting Bull to surrender. He met Brave Bear, who admitted to him that he had killed Johnson, and even told the scout where he had hidden Johnson's money. Allison bided his time, hoping to turn him in when the fugitives were back on the reservation.

For a month after the Sitting Bull band arrived at Fort Yates, Brave Bear was unmolested. Then, early in September, it was announced that the entire band would be taken as prisoners to Fort Randall. Sitting Bull raved and stormed, and threatened to fight to the death rather than go to Randall. A heavy guard was set about the camp, but at night some thirty Indians escaped. Among them was Brave Bear. Allison, pretending to help him escape, provided him with a knife and a revolver, and on the evening of September 6, put him in a canoe to get him across the Missouri, and off the reservation, where there the agency and military personnel had no jurisdiction.25 He took a risk in giving him weapons, but it was necessary to deceive the Indian.

About midnight, Brave Bear reached Louis Agard's ranch, where he tried to get a horse. When Agard refused the request, Brave Bear set off. Jake Houser, who was stopping overnight at the place feared that the criminal might murder someone to get a horse. He rounded up John Manning and Frank Sullivan, and trailed him to the house of the squawman, Andy Marsh. When they attempted to arrest him, he drew the revolver, but Marsh snatched it away, and the four men wrestled him to the floor and tied him up, while Marsh's wife and children crawled through a window and stayed outside until the struggle was over.

He imagined that they wanted to kill him, so he asked for a pipe and tobacco before they could dispatch him. They assured him, however, that they did not intend to execute him, but just turn him over to the civil authorities and collect the promised reward. The captive then became quite sociable, and put up little resistance. The next day he was taken to Bismarck and turned over to the United States Commissioner. It was at that very time that Major McLaughlin arrived at Bismarck on his way to become the new agent at Fort Yates.[26]

From Bismarck the Commissioner transferred Brave Bear to Yankton, the territorial capital, going on a train by way of St. Paul.

The indictment was for the murder of Joseph Johnson, to which Brave Bear pleaded not guilty on December 12. (No other crimes of Brave Bear were considered). The trial was held on January 5, 1882, and he was convicted without much delay. Then on January 9, Judge Alonzo J. Edgerton passed this sentence:

'Whereupon, all and singular, the premises being seen and by the said court fully understood, it is considered by the court here, and the judgement of the law being so, the sentence of the court is that you, Ma-to-o-hi-ti-ke, alias Wa-pe-pe, otherwise known in the English language as Brave Bear, be remanded hence to the place where you came; that you be there imprisoned until Thursday, the ninth day of March, A.D., 1882, upon which day will thence be conducted to the place of execution, where, between the hours of 9 o'clock in the forenoon and 2 o'clock in the afternoon of the said day, you shall be hanged by the neck until you shall be dead. And may the Lord have mercy on your soul.'[27]

Brave Bear's counsel, Oliver Shannon thereupon appealed to the supreme court for a new trial, and this action caused a delay, so that he was not hanged on the day appointed. The supreme court denied the appeal and ordered Judge Edgerton to set a new date for the execution. Accordingly, on May 26 he ordered that Brave Bear be hanged on July 20. At this juncture Bishop Martin Marty, O.S.B., and the Mercy Sisters at Yankton joined Judge Shannon in an appeal to the President to have the execution postponed sixty days. The delay was granted, and they secured a second sixty-day delay, while they worked hard to get the sentence commuted to imprisonment. Marty had served for some years as the founding missionary at Fort Yates and he understood the traumatic experience the Indians experienced in adjusting to the white men's ways and laws. He therefore sought to enlist the support of influential persons in his appeal for clemency toward Brave Bear. We quote in full here the letter he wrote to James McLaughlin, while not necessarily agreeing with the slighting remarks he made about Protestants:

Yankton   May 30, 82

J.M.J.
My dear Major,

 An Indian, who for a while lived at Standing Rock & for a time in the hostile camp - Brave Bear - has been accused of the murder of a white man, Clerk at the Cheyenne Agy, Mr. Johnson. It is on circumstantial evidence & on the fact established by revengeful and unreliable witnesses like Mr. Allison & other frontier men, that articles of the deceased were found in B.B.'s possession - whilst no attention is paid to the simple explanation of the same by the accused - that B. has been sentenced to death by a jury of frontiersmen, who as a general thing consider the Indian only so much vermin to be exterminated, whenever you get a chance.
 This act is in the eyes of the Indians & and of more thoughtful white men a breach of promises given, when the Indians in good faith surrendered to the whites & made a peace, the hostility public and private being condoned by both parties.
 You know how Indian young men are trained to consider the killing of their enemies & the stealing of his property a brave and honorable act: the sundance and its recitals in many places encouraged by Gov. officials, the paintings on their buffalo robes, the feathers & scalps in their dress repeating & inculcating the same lesson.
 If we think it just that ever God should judge every man in accordance with his conscience, how can we condemn an Indian before we have taught him by word and example the lessons of Christianity & formed in him a different kind of conscience?
 But this is precisely what heathenism & protestanism have always done, entice a man into sin & then rise up against him in pharisaical indignation like those to whom the Saviour said: If one of you is without sin let him cast the f. stone.
 Now Judge Oliver Shannon, B. B.'s counsel wishes to lay the case before the President & obtain a commutation of sentence. To make his appeal effective he wishes to obtain a number of letters from influential men in favor of justice and mercy & I think a few lines from you would be very serviceable. You may think of other men who would render us the same good office.

All these letters to the President should be sent to me, that they might be sent all together from here with the appeal of Judge Oliver Shannon to whose exposition of the case all the letters refer.

It will be known to the whole of the Sioux that B.B. owes his life to Catholic influence & that would also be an advantage.

May God's will in this thing as in every other be done & the salvation of our wards be advanced!

With many compliments to Mrs. McL., Mr. Faribault & friends, I am ever

       Yours truly
       M. Marty '28

Mc Laughlin strongly backed Bishop Marty in his appeal, as can be seen from his reply:

       'Standing Rock
       June 9th, 1882

Right Rev. Bishop,

Your letter of May 31st, ultimo, relative to the Indian prisoner "Brave Bear," now under sentence of death at Yankton for the murder of a white man in 1879, is just received, and in reply I desire to state that I am very well acquainted with Brave Bear, having known him since the spring of 1874. His father, mother, brother and sisters are living at this agency and are among the most obedient and best disposed Indians here, but "Brave Bear" is of a very different disposition, and to be acquainted with him is to know him to be capable of any mischief or misdemeanor and while I do not question his guiltiness of the crime for which he is condemned to death, yet I do consider it bad faith on the part of the late followers of "Sitting Bull," the hostile Indians were to be granted full amnesty for their past acts.

The arrest of "Brave Bear" was only a matter of speculation on the part of those effecting the same, he being induced by the Interpreter Allison to leave the reservation, when the arrest was made, with the hope of obtaining the reward that had been offered for him in 1879, and as before stated, while I do not doubt his guilt, yet there is a question involved which is of a serious enough nature to be worthy of careful consideration, that is, will it do for the best interests of the Indians in general or of the American people, that this Indian should be executed for a crime which from his education and training he did not consider of very grave nature, and should we, a powerful and civilized people exact from the untutored savage this stern obedience to our laws which protection we have refused them heretofore and which we have never acted to force upon them until now, without first preparing them by some warning or previous instruction. Why has not the Indian been first given to understand that in case of such a crime committed upon any person white or Indian, forfeiture of life would be the penalty?

The Indian schooling, by his tribal laws, has been that but to be prepared to meet the friends of his victim, or satisfaction in property, was all that was requisite and in view of these facts I trust that Executive clemency will be extended to this unfortunate criminal.

In this connection I desire to add that a special code for Indians in their semi-civilized condition should be made and if this cannot be secured, then I would urge that they be made amenable to all the laws that apply to the white man and the same be fully made known to them before they are launched into that which they have no conception of.

With my kindest regards, I have the honor to be,
Most respectfully,
Your obedient servant,
James McLaughlin
U.S. Indian Agt.[29]

Right Rev. M. Marty O.S.B.
Bishop of Dakota
Yankton, D.T.'

Two months later McLaughlin wrote to the Commissioner of Indian Affairs in the same vein and added: 'I am of the opinion that the interests of the government would be best served by a commutation of the death sentence to imprisonment for a term of years, by which justice may, in this case, be as well satisfied, and be an exhibition to the Indians of the magnanimity of the government in its efforts to civilize their race.'[30]

After both of the appeals headed by Marty failed, a third attempt was made by having the Sioux Commission join in the appeal, arguing that the execution of Brave Bear would anger the Indians and destroy the work of the Commission in its attempts to get the Standing Rock Indians to agree to their proposals. But President Arthur refused to concede, and on November 13, 1882, sent a telegram that the execution should be carried out. Gallows were quickly erected so as to be ready on November 16. Those who had worked futilely to save his life did not abandon him in his last moments, as is evident in this lengthy account taken from the *Yankton Weekly Press and*

Dakotian:

'He slept well last night and appeared much refreshed by the rest he received. He fully made up his mind that he must die today, but his nerve did not desert him. Putting the forefinger of each hand under his eyes, he said: "No water here." To jailor Kelly he gave a few directions. He wanted his pipe and tobacco put in the box with him when he was buried and he designated a few trinkets to be sent to his wife at Fort Randall. This was all and his instructions were given with the utmost calmness.

Father [Georg L.] Willard visited the doomed Indian in the jail at six o'clock this morning and held mass, the ceremony lasting three-quarters of an hour. Brave Bear sat upon his couch while the priest performed his solemn duty and listened attentively to the words he did not understand, but felt that they conveyed comfort during his last few hours of life and guaranteed a safe entrance into the beyond.

...After he had finished his breakfast two sisters of mercy glided into the jail and knelt beside the bed of Brave Bear. They remained about an hour engaged all the while in their devotions and in offering comfort to the Indian...

Twelve o'clock noon was the hour decided upon for the execution, but this information was not given out because the officers did not care to have a crowd about when the fatal moment arrived.

At Ten o'clock this forenoon, Marshal Allen placed guards about the jail to keep away the crowd and they remained on duty until after the execution. There was not much of a rush, but the disposition of those present was to mass themselves as closely as possible around the frail barricade which surrounded the scaffold. This Marshal Allen desired to prevent and he had the guards put around the premise.

About an hour set for the execution, Father Willard, accompanied by two sisters of mercy, went into the jail and took their accustomed positions along side the couch of Brave Bear. After a brief season of religious consolation the sisters retired, leaving Father Willard and an interpreter with the Indian, surrounded by the guard placed inside the room to watch the prisoner. A little after eleven o'clock the shackles were cut from Brave Bear's legs and for the first time since his incarceration he was permitted to dispense with his iron companions.

He appeared to enjoy his freedom and walked briskly about, talking and laughing. The priest remained his constant attendant and whenever opportunity offered gave him religious consolation. At half past eleven Brave Bear lighted his pipe and smoked briskly while conversing with his spiritual advisor. After finishing his smoke he arose, shook his legs as an indication he was relieved to be free from the irons and called for a drink, which was given him...Though the doomed Indian endeavored by every word and act to appear careless and unconcerned, it was evident that beneath all his forced calmness there was a nervousness he desired to conceal. Every movement of the bolts and every swing of a door caused him to start suddenly and turn his eyes in the direction of the sound. He was expecting the final summons and could not conceal his expectancy. Finally he made an effort to compose himself, took a seat upon his couch, accepted a proffered book from the priest and engaged in earnest conversation with him. But all the time he kept crossing and uncrossing his legs, pulling a handkerchief through one hand and then the other, and moving from side to side.

Finally he rose from his couch, walked briskly around the room, shook hands with the priest and the guards with a smile upon his face...About ten minutes before twelve District Attorney Palmer came into the jail and Brave Bear advanced to the grating to greet him, and extending his hand said, "good one." In a few words Brave Bear then asked Mr. Palmer to see to the disposition of a few private effects and some money he had. It was concealed in the ground near a tree at Standing Rock, and his father would know where to find it. He said his good wife (the one at Standing Rock) had the key to the box and he wanted her to have the money. His Fort Randall wife he said was bad. As near as Mr. Palmer could make out from his talk, the box contains about fifteen hundred dollars in gold. The conversation between the two was closed by Brave Bear, who said, "I want all white men to come and shake hands - that's good - then I am dead."

At five minutes before twelve the interview with the district attorney closed, and Brave Bear took a seat in a chair and laughingly conversed with Father Willard and the interpreter, all the time nervously extending his arms to full length, and at intervals wearily placing one hand upon his forehead. At last he bowed his head in earnest conversation with his priestly advisor and just then the noon bells began to ring. It was the signal that his last moment had almost arrived and guards and attendants stepped back, leaving the priest and the doomed

Indian in solemn communion for a few seconds. Brave Bear then arose and walked up and down the room, laughing loudly as he conversed with those about him.

Soon he was taken to the marshal's office, where the long document recalling his crime was read to him, and the sentence pronounced. He made no confession of his crime, but asked through his interpreter that word be sent to his people to make no attempt to avenge his death, to kill no horses and to omit all the customary mourning exercises. He also asked that the message he had sent to his people be conveyed to the President, that the great father might know he had given good advice. He then shook hands with all present, and walked the few steps to the gallows platform, where his arms and legs were bound, and a black hood placed over his head. The rope was placed around his neck and the awful moment had arrived.

...Brave Bear was beginning to weaken and it was necessary for a couple of officers to stand near to sustain him. In his nervous agitation he caught hold of the drooping rope as it swung in front of him and clung to it with the fingers of his pinioned hands. An officer released his hold and moved the rope back out of his reach. Then he stood, bound hand and foot, with his head covered by the black cap, awaiting the signal which was to send him to instant death. Father Willard advanced to his side, whispered a few words of prayer and then stepped back to the edge of the platform. The officer in charge pulled the string which rang the bell in the marshal's office. The man within the room, in response to the signal, jerked the rope attached to the trigger beneath the scaffold and at half past twelve o'clock the drop fell. The Indian shot through the opening and as the rope pulled taut there was a cracking sound. He struggled for a few moments, but the end came quickly. Soon there was nothing but the convulsive twitching of the muscles. In fifteen minutes from the time the drop fell Brave Bear was pronounced dead by the attending physicians. Fifteen minutes later the body was cut down and delivered to the undertaker, who caused it to be buried in the Catholic cemetery.[31]

The next day Red Shield sought out McLaughlin at Fort Yates.

'Is my son dead?' asked the father.

'He is dead,' the agent answered.

'Are you sure he is dead?' persisted the father.

'I have a telegram saying that he was hanged yesterday,'

replied McLaughlin.

'It is well,' replied Red Shield. 'We are glad, his mother and myself, for he was a bad son.' "[32]

The story of Brave Bear, by right, ought to end here, but there is much more that needs to be commented on concerning Mato Ohitika.

When this author first read the story of Brave Bear, the first thought was, what kind of person are we dealing with here? Was the "bad son" truly some sort of psychopath? Was he the bad seed? I read and reread the available information concerning Brave Bear and have come to some rather different conclusions. For one thing, we must remember the times in which Brave Bear lived. The Sioux wars (so-called from the American standpoint) had placed the Lakota/Dakota peoples in dire straits. These "wars" had started in 1862 in western Minnesota and did not really culminate until there was a final massacre of Indian people on a bleak and viciously cold day in 1890 at a desolate valley now known as Wounded Knee.

The buffalo that once roamed the plains had been decimated by trainloads of "sportsmen," and the good land of the Sioux that had been their domain was all gone. For those who had not escaped to Canada, there remained only the misery of the reservations. Hatred and enmity from the frontier interlopers and the misconception of the Indian as an uncivilized savage or barbarian were common themes in the literature of the day. One gets a very excellent glimpse of this so-called literature in such books as McConkey's, "Dakota War Whoop/or Indian Massacres and War in Minnesota/of 1862-3," and in W. Fletcher Johnson's "The Red Record of the Sioux/Life of Sitting Bull and History of the Indian War of 1890-91." All the Indian hate epithets and ethnic misrepresentations are contained in these two examples of hate literature. And, as if this undercurrent is not enough, there is the corruption of historical fact that is part and parcel of books of this sort. Just as the first settlers in the Americas utilized the theme that the original peoples were sub-human brutes to justify extermination, slavery, and other ills that were used to dull the collective conscience, so this same sort of propaganda was used against the nomadic buffalo hunters of the great plains.

Brave Bear was the product of his times. In the "Brave Bear Murder Case," Brave Bear is said to have killed some thirty Sioux. However, there is no corroboration for this comment, and it is really not such a surprising comment from that era that such a charge was put forth. The great Oglala Lakota chief, Red Cloud (Mahpia Luta) was said to have counted coup over sixty times in his lifetime. Thus, the stage was set to show that these men were unprincipled murderers; sub-human and thus worthy of being removed from life on this earth. It should also be explained at this point in the narrative that the culture of the Lakota/Dakota peoples placed more emphasis (thus a greater pride) in touching an enemy in battle then in actually killing a warrior. This touching of an enemy was effected by touching the person with a coup stick, and thus it was called "counting coup." Certainly it is possible that Brave Bear may have counted coup on the enemies of his people during those turbulent years on the plains, but had he killed members of his own people, he certainly would have been killed in turn by family members of the deceased. In numerous warrior societies, he would have been allowed to offer restitution to the affected families; if that was not acceptable, then his life would have been forfeit to any member of the family.

Brave Bear is also noted acting as a procurer of women for mean purposes to the various white riffraff who lived at the various forts and agencies. This type of comment was meant to inflame the better class of people who tried to set up a decent society based on Christian mores. There is, however, no written documentation to sustain this allegation. And, if Brave Bear actually acted the part of the pimp, then he was no worse then his Euro-American contemporaries who were voracious in taking Indian women into prostitution. This does not absolve Brave Bear by any means of such inhuman behavior, but again, the record is only hearsay.

Next, we must look at the De Lorme murders. Brave Bear was never actually tried for these crimes, although the facts are indisputable that he and his gang surely committed the crime. Still, there are some strange points to be looked at in connection with this crime. What about Langis, the man who Brave Bear really wished to avenge himself upon? Certainly this Langis must be considered as an accomplice. Why would he point out the home of the De Lorme's family to the Indians? He could easily have invented some story that the man who Brave Bear was looking for had moved to some other location, or some other such story. Again, we are told that Brave Bear, The Only One et al entered into the "Chippewa settlements." If these were indeed settlements as we can envision them, why didn't Langis sound the alarm. He knew Brave Bear and he certainly knew his intentions. Perhaps this Langis should have also been called into a court of law to explain his actions or lack thereof. Still, we cannot absolve Wapepe of his deeds. The eyewitness testimony of the survivors is more then enough to judge him, by law, as being guilty of a heinous crime. I find one other problem with this event - why would Captain Bell, who had charge of Brave Bear at Fort Totten write to Van Etten with the notion that he wanted to set Brave Bear free? It's true that Bell had a problem for space in the guardhouse, and also quite probable that there might have been some dissatisfaction among his Indian charges at Fort Totten, but we are talking here about a man who was adjudged to be a murderer. Was Brave Bear some kind of a con artist to so sway Captain Bell? One may never know.

The crime for which Brave Bear eventually was tried and executed was the murder of Joseph Johnson. In this day and age a competent defense attorney would easily have been able to obtain a verdict of not guilty. The dictums of U.S. jurisprudence were definitely not followed during the trial. Still, this does not mean that Brave Bear was some kind of an innocent. That he killed Johnson seems sure, but the law doesn't always weigh her scales of justice the way we think. The idea that a man is considered innocent until proven guilty did not apply to any Indian, let alone Brave Bear. When our "bad son" left for Canada and joined the band of Sitting Bull, he most likely, unwittingly set the stage for an adept attorney to have him set free and absolved of his crimes. One of the assurances given the Sitting Bull contingent to return from Canada was that all members of the band would be given a general amnesty. This amnesty would have, and, in law, should have applied to Brave Bear.

There are other inconsistencies in the Brave Bear story. What about Edwin H. "Fish" Allison? On the evening when some thirty of Sitting Bull's people escaped from the camp after their surrender, why would he give Brave Bear a gun, some funds, and take him across the Missouri in a canoe? First, when he did such a thing, it had to be with the idea of later capturing Brave Bear off the reservation and collecting reward monies. He also had to know that others of the Sitting Bull band intended to escape. Why didn't he simply alert the U.S. Army authorities? "Fish" Allison, by his reckless conduct almost caused a number of innocent people to be killed by Brave Bear, and his actions, to me, seem unconscionable. In looking briefly at Edmund Allison, it is also relevant that he was the man who claimed later in life that he alone was responsible for the surrender of Sitting Bull and his band.[33] Finally, while on the subject of Allison, I find the remarks of Bishop Martin Marty quite revealing when he commented on him as being "revengeful & unreliable..." Perhaps Marty knew more about this scout and interpreter then has been recorded in our histories of the man. It's too bad, in a way, that Bishop Marty did not elaborate more concerning Allison. And, seeing as how his letter was addressed to James McLaughlin, this agent must certainly have known much concerning his character. Alas for McLaughlin, upon receiving Bishop Marty's appeal, he was placed in a position which must have been somewhat difficult for him. McLaughlin was Roman Catholic and thus must have felt obligated to the Bishop to respond affirmatively to the call for clemency. And there is also, as I read Marty's letter a certain "ring" about the clemency appeal..., it's as if the good Bishop might have been more concerned with proselytizing and/or extending the offices of the missionaries among the Lakota/Dakota people. Certainly, the comment about "protestants" was uncalled for, but, in the days of Bishop Marty and for many years afterward, such prejudicial remarks were common among almost all Christian communities.

There is one final point which I will touch upon concerning Brave Bear. He was said to have been somewhat of an outcast among his own people. It's probably true that his presence in various camps brought forth the ire of various military or agency personnel, but to say that he was an unwelcome guest certainly belies the facts. The Cut Heads had refused to give him up, except under duress from the army and he seemed to travel and live among numerous of his people in their camps in a rather amicable fashion. But the telling question; the most damning accusation that ever faced Mato Ohitika occurred after his death. It is difficult over the pages of time to read the relation as originally given by McLaughlin concerning the deceased. The father, Red Shield, who commented, "FOR HE WAS A BAD SON!" What a very sad epitaph!

NOTES

1. The translation for Wapepe was furnished by the State Historical Society of North Dakota from a translation by Siouxan speaker Mary Louis Defender Wilson. This information was courtesy of Virginia Heidenreich, Managing Editor of North Dakota History. Letter to the author, dated March 8, 1989.
2. Burdick, Usher L. (ed.). My Friend the Indian; or Three Heretofore Unpublished Chapters of the Book Published Under the Title of My Friend the Indian. Baltimore, 1936.
3. Lt. Col. L.C. Hunt to A.A.G., Dept. of Dakota, National Archives Record Group 98, Records of the U.S. Army Commands, Fort Totten, Letters Sent, July 19, 1874.
4. Idem. there is some doubt as to whether The Only One was a member of the gang at this time. Pretty Dog seems to have been the fourth member of the quartet.
5. Idem.
6. Belleau Collection, Assumption Abbey Archives.
7. Captain J.S. Naught to the Post Commander at Fort Pembina, National Archives Record Group 98, Records of the U.S. Army Commands, Fort Totten, Letters Received, July 8, 1874.
8. *The Turtle Mountain Star*, Jan. 26, 1950.
9. *The Fargo Forum*, March 4, 1946, an article by Roy P. Johnson. The letter cited in footnote 3 supports this statement.
10. *The Bismarck Tribune*, November 25, 1874.
11. Idem, December 30, 1874.
12. *The Westerners Brand Book* (Chicago Corral), September, 1960, p. 51.
13. Hughes to Carlin, October 29, 1877, cited in E.A. Mulligan's unpublished thesis (U. of N. Dak.), "The Standing Rock Sioux, 1874-1890," p. 77.
14. Frances Chemberlein (sic - Chamberlein) Holley, *Once Their Home* (Chicago, 1890), p. 335.
15. Major James McLaughlin Papers, Assumption Abbey Archives.
16. James McLaughlin, *My Friend the Indian* (Boston, 1910), p. 43.
17. Major James McLaughlin Papers, Assumption Abbey Archives.
18. Don Patton to Roy P. Johnson, December 19, 1941, Johnson Collection, Assumption Abbey Archives, Ben Ash File.
19. Major James McLaughlin Papers, Assumption Abbey archives.
20. McLaughlin, *My Friend the Indian*, p. 50. George Parker wrote several letters to McLaughlin trying to find his stolen horse.
21. Major James McLaughlin Papers, Letterbook 1878-1881, pp. 296, 311-312.
22. Same reference as in note 18. Ash later became U.S. Indian Agent in that area, and was in a position to get accurate accounts. One account states that Brave Bear traveled along with Johnson for a way, then shot

him in the back. It is hard to tell which version is the true one.
23. Holley, *Once Their Home*, pp. 336-37. The Grey Nun's Journal (St. Michael, N. Dak.) records the scare on May 31, 1879.
24. Holley, *Once Their Home*, p. 337.
25. *The Bismarck Tribune*, September 9, 1881.
26. Idem; Mrs. William Taylor, a daughter of Marsh, years later recalled the exciting episode: "My father got him and tied him down with a rope & took him to Bismarck for the reward which was $200.00 that he never got for some reason. ... I remember that night my dad got him. My mother and us kids were so scared we went through the window and hid out in the dark till it was over." - Andrew Marsh File, Johnson Collection, Assumption Abbey Archives: In his book *My Friend the Indian*, (p. 51), McLaughlin attributes Brave Bear's flight from the reservation to his arrival on the scene, but this is not what actually happened, for the new agent arrived at Fort Yates a few days after the capture.
27. *Yankton Weekly Press and Dakotian*, Nov 16, 1882.
28. Major James McLaughlin Papers, Assumption Abbey Archives.
29. Major James McLaughlin Papers, Assumption Abbey Archives.
30. Major James McLaughlin papers, Assumption Abbey archives, September 1, 1882.
31. *Yankton Weekly Press and Dakotian*, Nov. 16, 1882.
32. McLaughlin, *My Friend the Indian*, p. 40. The *Fargo Daily Argus*, Nov. 29, 1882, contained this article: "Bismarck Tribune: Major McLaughlin, Indian agent at standing Rock, returned last evening from St. Paul. At Fargo Sheriff Haggart gave him the saber used by Brave Bear in the murder of the DeLong [De Lorme] family in Pembina county in 1874. this saber has been in the hands of the court since the murder, but now that Brave Bear has gone to the happy hunting grounds, the court has no more use for it, and Major McLaughlin will keep it as a souvenir of the noted chief."
33. Dowd, James P. *Custer Lives!* Fairfield, Wash., 1982, p. 58. Entry # 8.

CHAPTER 5

GHOST DANCE WOMAN

Wananikwe - I call her Ghost Dance Woman. She was a prophetess (and some claim the Blessed Virgin) who preceded Wovoka, the Nevada Pauite by nearly a decade. To those unfamiliar with Wovoka, it was he who prophesied the return of a Messiah and the eventual salvation of the Original Peoples. The message he gave was surrounded with various rituals which were intended to ensure the return of the ancestors of the Original People and which would return the ways of old to a terribly demoralized and desperate people. An American misconception and Lakota Sioux corruption of his Ghost Dance ended with the last great massacre of the Original People on this continent in 1891. The message of Wananikwe was eerily identical, yet those who received her message managed to avoid massacre and have maintained her message into the present day. Instead of the Ghost Dance, she initiated what was known as the "Sioux dance," and what today is called "Big Drum." "Big Drum" is sacred and the ceremonies are not open to outsiders. Thus, it is that I am constrained in naming all my sources for this brief saga of Wananikwe.

SANTEE DAKOTA (SIOUX)

WANANIKWE - Stranger Woman. There is no known year of birth or death of this woman. She simply entered the pages of history in 1876 like some great bolt of lightning, and once the sound of her thunder passed she simply disappeared into the eastern sky. Did she really exist as a true human being? Or was she simply the spirit which entered into the hearts and souls of a people whose entire existence and culture was being decimated? She was definitely a real human being, and yes, she did arrive in the north country of Wisconsin bringing with her a message of a Messiah.

Among the few notable anthropologists who have ever mentioned her were Barrett (1911), Landes (1970), and Clifton (1977). Considering the importance of the cultural impact that Wananikwe had in the late 1800's and continues to have among numerous tribal groups today, she deserves to be known. And perhaps her "real" message should be heard by all peoples. This is not just history. This story of a prophetess is perhaps germane to the entire gamut of spirituality which has existed in the elemental being of mankind since the beginning of time. Hear then, what little is written about her in the historical record, and hear further the story I have been privileged to hear of her from those who have told me something of her and her message as it exists today.

THE BIG DRUM IS PAINTED RED. THIS SIGNIFIES THE PASSION AND DESPAIR OF JESUS CHRIST. THE DRUM LEADER IS TRANSFORMED INTO JESUS CHRIST AND HE SENDS HIS MESSAGES TO THE GREAT FATHER WHO LOVES ALL MEN.

Clifton[1] has recorded that the first mention of Wananikwe occurred in 1876 among the Prairie Band of the Potawatomi Nation in Kansas, and that by 1883 the new religion had been accepted and was being practised by them. Agent Linn and his successor I.W. Patrick expressed a great deal of tolerance for the new religion, with only one exception, that being, that these profoundly poor reservation people spent an inordinate amount of time in the dances. Linn remarked that "...the moral tendency was very good, as the teaching was in accord with the Ten Commandments." The message that the Prairie Potawatomi received spoke out against the abuses of alcohol, adultery, gambling and murder. According to Clifton the message received by the Prairie Band was conveyed to them by messengers from the Ojebwe and Potawatomi of Wisconsin. But, the traditional story given by the northern Great Lakes people is far different. It is a mystical relation. The word was brought to the Potawatomi of the plains in a mystical manner.[2]

"When all the people were gathered about the drum one day and singing, a light appeared in the distance. At first the people paid no attention to this light. But soon, the light began to grow very bright, and, in the midst of the light, a beautiful woman dressed in white buckskin appeared. She told the people she was pleased with their drum and their singing and told them to continue this for all time, as it pleased her Father to hear their praises to him." The instructions that followed also included directions on how the drum was to be decorated and new songs were given to those who were in attendance. This is the story I have been told. Is it something that a modern day man can offer credence to? Who cares! The technological world we live in will certainly say no, but the inner person within all human beings will at least think that it may have really been a manifestation of that which governs all the universe.

When next we hear of Wananikwe and the Dream Dance, it is from agent E. Stephens at Keshena, Wisconsin.[3] Agent Stephens was certainly disturbed by the results of Wananikwe's visions as he wrote two letters to the Office of Indian Affairs on the same day, August 23, 1881 The first letter is as follows:

"Hon Comr of Indian Affairs
               Washington DC
Sir

The Indians belonging to the Menominee reservation who have been engaged in the dance known as the Sioux dance have for the past two days been reinforced by a delegation of about forty western Indians Pottawatomies and Chippewas who have come on to the reservation for the purpose of putting new life into and keeping up said dance.

They tell the Indians that at some future day, a great drum will tap in heaven, and at that time all the whites and Catholic Indians will be paralized(sic), when all they have to do is to walk forth and tap them on the head - and take possession of the land. Your Agent together with the Chiefs of the Menominee tribe, on learning of their presence, visited them and ordered them to leave the reservation, but they refused to go, and went on with their dancing; they are here for the purpose of getting new recruits from the young men of the Menominee tribe, and are determined to keep up said dance, much to the detriment of the Menominee Indians. Please see my telegram 'scout'(?) this evening asking for aid in this matter.

      Very Respectfully
      E. Stephens
      U.S. Indian Agent"

 The second letter of the same date hurriedly followed, and Stephens was seemingly either exasperated or fearful of some dire consequences of what was happening...:

"Hon Comr of Indian Affairs
   Washington DC
Sir

Referring to your letters dated January 20th and June 14th 1881 'Cir'. When I am instructed to inform the Indians of this Agency, that if they continue to engage in the dance known as the Sioux dance, 'All their annuities of goods and moneys will be withheld so long as they continue to indulge in the objectionable practise.'

In reply to the above, I would state that at the last annuity payment (made June 17th 1881) I read your letters to the Indians and had the same fully interpreted to them, and as the members of the dance above referred to came forward for their money, I required them to take an oath that they would abandon the said dance and use their utmost influence to break up the same, a few of the Indians refused to take their money, and the same was transferred to the credit of the U.S. at the close of the fiscal year 1881.

Since that time most of the Indians who were members of said dance have returned to the same, and still continue. They have lately been reinforced by outside Indians and are neglecting their crops, in some cases letting them go to destruction. At the present time they have been dancing for three or four days and are still at it, they claim that the instructions which I have recited to them did not come from Washington, but were manufactured here at the Agency, this they pretend to believe, and pay no attention to the orders of their Chiefs or your Agent - please note my letter and telegram of even date herewith, advising you of the intrusion by outside Indians and send me full instructions as to dealing with the Menominee leaders of said dance.

      Very Respectfully
      E. Stephens

U.S. Indian Agent"

It has been alleged that Wananikwe first brought the Sioux Dance to the Menominee, and that she was a slave who had been taken in a raid by the Menominee against the Santee Sioux. However, the Menominee make no such claims. Instead, Wananikwe appeared first among the Potawatomi of northern Wisconsin, and not as a slave, but as a refugee. When I first mentioned the name of this mystical woman to friends among the Wisconsin Potawatomi, the initial reaction was one of denial. This was not at all surprising as most original peoples can claim to have a spirituality that has secret rites, visions and other elements that allow these peoples to assert their own cultural individuality. And such mystical knowledge is passed on only from knowledgeable individuals to others who are considered spiritually acceptable. Thus the story I now give of Wananikwe is all that can be given of her, and still maintain a cultural/spiritual balance which will allow the original peoples their last refuge in the ways of the ancestors. THUNDER IS A GOOD SPIRIT!

They say[4] that Wananikwe was born about 1839. While still a young woman and unmarried, her Dakota village came under attack by enemies. She made her escape to a shallow lake, and immediately dove into the water, and taking a reed for breathing, she concealed herself for four days. (Note-this number four is in accord with the four principle directions) At the end of the four days, the enemy departed and she was given a vision. The Great Spirit appeared to her dressed in a fine white buckskin garment. He glowed all over. And he began to tell her and teach her the words of various songs. She was told to go to the people of the east - the Potawatomi, Menominee and Chippewa and tell them the songs and teachings he gave to her. This was the beginning of the "Big Drum."

The teachings of Wananikwe were dutifully given to the Potawatomi of Wisconsin, and soon spread to the Menominee, Chippewa, Ottawa, Kickapoo, Sac and Fox. What started in a small community in northern Wisconsin soon spread throughout Minnesota, Kansas, Iowa, and Oklahoma. Today, the Big Drum is one of the major spiritual and ceremonial religions of the original peoples of the Great Lakes and the southern plains states. And yet, Wananikwe, the founder, is virtually unknown outside of Native American communities. Aside from her original revelations, there are no "miracles" ascribed to her, nor is there any information about her except what can be gathered from the original people. Wananikwe is an enigma. She was called by one informant, White Buffalo Calf Woman, but this name does not translate as such. When I first mentioned the name to an elder from Odanah in northern Wisconsin, he momentarily became extremely alert, and simply called out, "Ah, the old woman!" It is best for those are not Original People to ask few questions concerning spirituality... Wananikwe is "Strange Woman" to be sure. She entered this world silently and left this world silently. Perhaps the Thunders carried her off, or perhaps Eagle carried her to her final reward. We may never know.

NOTES:

1. Clifton, James A. The Prairie People: Continuity and Change in Potawatomi Indian Culture 1665-1965. The Regents Press of Kansas, Lawrence, (1977).
2. Northern Potawatomi informants - 1991.
3. Records of the Bureau of Indian Affairs - Letters Received 1881-1907, #15282.
4. Northern Potawatomi informants - 1991.

CHAPTER 6

THE IDAHO GIANT

What a title for a chapter in a book about our original peoples! Yet, the giant that you will meet in this story is indeed spectacular in many ways. His size and reputed endurance strike wonder in our minds.

His evil deeds throughout his brief life will perhaps tend to make him seem like unto some malevolent devil. Be that as it may, he was a human being; a human being with dreams, desires, hatreds and lurking in the background of his psyche was that somewhat strange and perhaps immutable thing which is part of what every human soul on this earth has in common. Through the misty windows of life, whether good or bad, all have somewhere, somehow, experienced LOVE.

In this wise, our Idaho giant was no different. Read now, the story of yet another person whose life was lived in the eye of a thunderstorm.

CHEROKEE - EUROAMERICAN - AFRO AMERICAN (PAIUTE BY ASSOCIATION)

Idaho Giant! Surely this is a strange name for an Indian. Well, it really wasn't his name at all. It's simply a descriptive device used to introduce the reader to a man who was born in the Cherokee Nation, the son of a Euro-American man named Archer Wilkinson and a mother who was part Cherokee and part Afro-American. He was christened Starr Wilkinson, and he claimed that he was so named after Thomas Starr, a noted desperado in the Nation.[1] But Starr Wilkinson, who was probably born about the year 1826, was much better known in later life as Bigfoot from the enormous size of his feet. Among the Paiute people who he eventually lived with, he was called Chief Nampuh, for which the city of Nampa, Idaho is presently named.[2] The story of Bigfoot was first recorded in the *Idaho Statesman* newspaper on November, 1878. Much of it, I fear, may be at best, only apocryphal. The story was sent to the Idaho newspaper by a man named William T. Anderson of Fisherman's Cove, California who was presumably a former resident of Idaho.

According to Anderson, Bigfoot gave a recital of his life as he lay dying in 1868 - a rather lengthy recital considering the man had received twelve rounds from a Henry rifle and lay bleeding to death. Bigfoot told about his family, a bit about his youth and a story of unrequited love. The story as told by Bigfoot is as follows: "The boys always made fun of me when I was a boy, because I was so large for my age, and had such big feet. I had a bad temper, and got to drinking when quite young, and got to be so strong that when anyone would call me a nickname I would fight him. In this way I came near killing several with my fist. I found out that I would soon be killed if I remained in that country, so I ran away from home, and went to Tiloqua [sic - Talequah], then the capital of the Cherokee nation. There I fell in with some emigrants, who were going to Oregon in 1856, and drove a team across the plains, for my board. The folks I traveled with were very kind to me. I fell in love with a young lady of the company, who thought a good deal of me until we fell in with a company from New York. Along with these new people was an artist, who was a smart, good looking fellow. He soon cut me out. After this the young lady would hardly notice me or speak to me. I knew then that he had told her something bad about me. He made fun of me several times, and, while we were camped near the Goose Creek Mountains, he and I went out one morning to hunt up the stock. We went to the bank of the Snake River. I asked him what he intended to do (with her?) when he got to Oregon. [Somehow there seems to be a sentence missing in all the narrations at this point - The premise is that the artist must have told Wilkinson that he intended to marry the young girl]. I told him he should not do so, for I thought I had the best right to her. He only laughed and said, 'Do you suppose she would marry a big-footed nigger like you, and throw off a good-looking fellow like me?' This made me mad, and I told him I was no negroe, and that if he called me that again I would kill him. So he drew his gun on me, and repeated it again. I was unarmed, but started at him. He shot me in the side but did not hurt me much, so I grabbed him and threw him down, and choked him to death, then threw him into the Snake River, took his gun, pistol, and knife, and ran off into the hills.'[3]

Upon leaving this scene of murder, Bigfoot headed into the wilderness, where he soon arrived at the camp of a man named Joe Lewis, who had lived with the Indians for many years. This man Lewis is supposed to have been one of the leading spirits involved in the Whitman Massacre of 1847 near Walla Walla, Washington. And thus, Bigfoot started his sojourn among the renegade Indians of west-central Idaho. He claimed to have gone with Lewis and his newly found Indian friends to rob the emigrants along the Old Fort Hall Road. In one of these raids, he supposedly recognized some cattle which belonged to the family who had originally taken him west from Talequa in the then Indian Territory. Bigfoot now decided to go to the train and try to get his girl to run off with him. He was confronted with the accusation that they were sure that he had killed the artist, a Mr. Hart. Bigfoot swore revenge if the girl would not go with him, but his party was not then strong enough to assault the emigrant train. He left, but his mind was filled only with thoughts of revenge. With Joe Lewis and a picked band of some thirty Indians, Bigfoot followed the train down the Boise River, attacked the train and massacred all, including the girl he claimed to have so ardently loved. Bigfoot went on to recite only two of the many other murders he had committed; the Scott family on Burnt River, and an unnamed officer on his way to Camp Lyon with a pregnant wife. The captured woman, he claimed, became weak after giving birth, and was dispatched by the other Indians.[4]

Remember, if you will, that all that has been said concerning Bigfoot up to this point was supposedly spoken as he lay dying. Not to be outdone, he didn't stop at what has already been related, but continued with his sanguine "history." Bigfoot gave as reason for his further misdeeds the fact that his Indian wife was killed, and his child taken away by a militia officer named Jefferson Stanford. Bigfoot then commented, "Since that time I have done all the mischief I could, and am glad of it."[5] And commit mischief, Big Foot certainly did! He and his desperate band of trusty followers infested the Idaho Territory and roamed the area from the Grand Ronde Valley in eastern Oregon to the heads of the Owyhee and Weiser rivers in present day Idaho. It was said that while other members of his band were mounted on horseback, Bigfoot always traveled on foot. It was proposed that perhaps no ordinary Indian pony could carry his reputed enormous hulk. As if to illustrate this, our author, William T. Anderson narrated the following:

"One day his fresh tracks would be seen on the Weiser, and the next day he would be heard of on the Owyhee, seventy-five or eighty miles distant.

One day he was chased by Wheeler [John M.], Frank Johnson, and a man by the name of Cook, who were all well mounted, while Bigfoot, as usual, was traveling on foot with two other Indians. Wheeler and his companions were camped near the head of the Malheur River. In the night their horses gave indications that Indians were prowling near the camp, so a close watch was kept up till daylight, when, on examination of the ground, it was discovered that old Bigfoot and two other Indians had been within a few yards of the camp during

the night. Upon making this discovery all were excited - all were eager for the chase. Bigfoot had been treading on dangerous ground. Here were three as cool and determined men as ever put a foot out West, all three of them crack marksmen, and all were accustomed to Indian fighting, and three better horsemen could not be found in the Territory.

Dispatching a hasty breakfast, all mounted their horses and took the trail, Frank Johnson remarking, 'Well, boys, we will make it hot for old Bigfoot today.' Wheeler replied laughingly, 'Yes; and it will make it hot for our horses to catch up with that old feather-headed devil, if he can travel as far as Enoch Fruit says he can.' Enoch Fruit was a noted horse thief, who once kept a ferry at Farewell Bend, on Snake River, and he had often met Bigfoot and often talked and traded with him. It was through Fruit that the fact was known that Bigfoot could speak English, and that it came to be believed that the big-footed fiend belonged to some other tribe of Indians than the one he was with, which in time proved to be true.

The three men rode on in hot pursuit. A fierce ride of two hours brought them in sight of the Indians, who were going in a rapid trot towards Snake River. All hands now prepared in earnest for the chase. The big Spanish spurs were applied without mercy to the already bleeding flanks of their faithful and spirited horses. The two smaller Indians were soon overtaken and shot down. They made a determined and desperate resistance, but their horses and arrows and old-style guns proved to no avail before the Henry rifle in the hands of the men they had now to deal with. By the time these two Indians were dispatched, old Bigfoot was at least a mile ahead, running and jumping the sagebrush like a deer, increasing the distance between him and his pursuers where the ground was the roughest, and losing where the ground was better. The exciting chase was kept up in this way for over thirty miles with about the same result, until at last the huge monster reached Snake River and plunged into the stream, and struck out swimming for the opposite shore. He proved himself to be an excellent swimmer, as well as a skillful runner, carrying his gun and ammunition above water. The faithful horses were now put down to their best speed, but only reached the bank in time for their riders to see, much to their disappointment and disgust, the tall form of Bigfoot clambering out of the water on the other bank. Johnson shouted out, 'Boys, look here; don't Bigfoot beat hell?' Cook said, 'Yes; and he beat our horses too.' Wheeler quietly remarked that if old Bigfoot did not have the rheumatism after running so far and then swimming that cold river, he deserved to be remembered as a living specimen of health and endurance.

In the meantime Bigfoot, having gained the bank of the river, and shaken himself, and after giving an unearthly yell, shouted out in plain English, 'Come over, come over, you d__d cowards,' and then dived into the thick willows..., It was, of course, owing to rocky gullies and rough ground that Bigfoot made his wonderful escape."[6]

Ah, come on guys, give the big boy a little credit! Anyone who could outrun three, armed, mounted men across some thirty miles of any kind of terrain, and then, like some superhuman being jump into the icy cold, swift running Snake River; swim the raging torrent (with his gun and ammunition held high) certainly deserves some better press than this! If Bigfoot actually managed to do all the things which only one man, William T. Anderson, claimed, he was indeed the wonder of any age. Lord, just think what kind of a salary he could have demanded from a modern day pro football team? Maybe even a pro wrestler yet? I guess I'm becoming somewhat facetious at this point, so it's best that I continue on with our narrative.

The man who was eventually credited with killing Bigfoot certainly had a checkered past himself, according to the 1878 original newspaper account. Of course, finding any record of John M. Wheeler is like searching for needles in a haystack. He was supposedly mixed up in an attempt to rob a stagecoach in the Blue Mountains in the autumn of 1868 (the same year in which he killed Bigfoot?). One would have thought he would have been granted hero status for his act of frontier gallantry. At any rate, it was said that he was captured and sentenced to ten years in the Oregon penitentiary. He was released in 1877, "conveniently" moved himself to California and later committed suicide.

The death of Bigfoot as given by Anderson is high melodrama at best, but as a thrilling story I dare not omit it from this story as my readers might well want to finish me off.

Even the holy devil of Russia, Rasputin, died easier than did Nampuh. Bigfoot was to fight his last fight in the latter part of July, 1868. Anderson, who claimed to have been on the scene, and just by happenstance have a measuring tape with him related the story: "I was going from Silver City to Boise City, traveling alone with a two-horse wagon. When near the dangerous pass where so many had been been killed, I, *being unarmed*, [author's italics] concluded to lay over and let my horses graze until I should have company through the canyon, so I foolishly turned my horses loose and set myself to cooking something to eat. While thus engaged, the horses got frightened at something and run off, leaving me afoot and alone, and badly frightened. I followed the horses' tracks, and found they had gone down Reynolds Creek, in the direction of the massacre ground. As the creek runs through this bluff of rocks within half a mile of where the road does, I followed them, and found that they had started through the canon, and I had just turned back, afraid to go farther, when, to my horror and surprise, I looked across the creek and saw three Indians coming at full speed. They were painted and feathered, and, as they were coming directly toward me, I felt certain that they saw me, and I thought that my time had come. The tall and terrible-looking Indian who could be none other than Bigfoot himself was some fifty yards ahead of another Indian, while the third was an equal distance behind the second one. I stood paralyzed with fear. The only chance left me was to hide behind some rocks, and there await my fate, which I felt certain would in a few minutes be death; so I crouched down behind a ledge of rocks, and bid a last farewell to home and friends, as I then thought, expecting that in a few minutes my dripping scalp would be hanging to the belt of the most horrible-looking monster I had ever beheld. It would useless for me to attempt to describe my feelings at this moment. In less than a minute old Bigfoot came thundering along like an old buffalo bull, within less than thirty yards of me, but did not halt, making straight for the road, which was not far off. I looked and saw the stage full of passengers, with several females among the number, just coming in sight.

    Somewhat to my relief I now discovered that it was the stage and not myself that was the object of Bigfoot's attention. He had evidently resolved to head off the stage, and murder the driver and rob the passengers. He was destined however to do no more scalping on this side of the 'dark river.' When the Indian who was next to the side of the chief was nearly opposite my hiding-place, my blood was chilled by the crack of a rifle, which dropped the Indian dead within twenty yards of me. At the report of the gun old Bigfoot jumped behind a large rock, and the hindmost Indian broke back over the hill and was not seen again. For a moment all was quite. I saw Charley Barnes throw the silk gracefully to his horses, as was his habit on nearing the canon; he and his his passengers all unconscious of the terrible fate they had just escaped. I afterwards learned that among the passengers were Judge Roseborough, Charley Douglass, the gambler, and Mrs. Record and her daughter. Mrs. Record and family were then keeping the stage station at the Fifteen-mile House, between Boise City and Snake River. Little did they think that there was one so near them as I was, and in such a terrible plight, who dared not move or ask for aid, and that the most deadly and bloody encounter was about to take place that had ever been witnessed by any of us. Those few minutes seemed like hours to me. I knew that an Indian had been killed near me, but by whom, or from what direction, I could form no idea. From Bigfoot's action it was evident that he thought the report of the gun came from a tree surrounded by a clump of willows near the creek, some eighty yards from where he stood. The sequel proved that he was right. A few minutes after the stage pulled out of sight, Bigfoot commenced practising a bit of strategy that was new to me. All I could do was to lie still and in dead silence watch his movements. First he would crawl from one side of the large rock behind which he was hiding, then crawl back to the other side and cautiously peep around the side of the rock; but no one shot at him. All was dead quietude. He would then put his ear to the ground and listen, but could not hear the slightest noise. At last he tried another plan of escape. He tied a large bunch of sagebrush to his back and tried to crawl away; and to my great horror he was advancing directly towards the spot where I lay hidden behind a ledge of rocks. He came slowly and gently towards me. I was undecided whether to remain where I was a while longer, or jump and run toward the clump of willows which Bigfoot had been watching so long, and take the chances of finding a white man. If I remained where I was much longer, Bigfoot, who had not yet seen me, could not fail to find me; but this terrible state of suspense was soon brought to an end.

When Bigfoot had crawled over about half the distance that separated his hiding-place from mine, I heard a clear voice ring out on the mountain air, in cool, deliberate tones. saying, 'Get up from there, Bigfoot, you old feather-headed, leather-bellied coward. I can see you crawling off like a snake. This is one time that you did not even get a woman's scalp. Here is a scalp: come down and take mine, you coward.' At this Bigfoot sprang to his feet, and leveled a large, double-barreled rifle at the willows, and said, 'You coward; me no coward. You come out; I'll scalp you too.' At this Wheeler sprang out from among the bushes in plain view, saying, 'Here I am, now sail in old rooster.' Both men fired at almost the same instant. Bigfoot staggered, but recovered and fired again, and then threw his gun down and started to run towards the dead Indian. He ran but a few yards, when another shot caused him to reel again, but he succeeded in reaching the spot where the dead Indian lay, and, picking up the gun left by the latter where he had fallen, he leveled it toward Wheeler and fired again, just at the moment that Wheeler's gun sent another unerring bullet into his powerful frame. Bigfoot again staggered and came very near falling, but again recovered, and, drawing a knife, gave an unearthly whoop, which almost froze my blood, and then started toward Wheeler. He had gone but a few yards when another shot staggered him, and then another. I was dumb with fear, apprehending that after all the Indian might succeed in reaching Wheeler and then grasp him in his powerful clutches. Wheeler never moved from the spot where he stood, but, handling his gun with extraordinary skill, continued to fire, until at last, when within thirty yards of him, the huge red demon fell with a broken leg to rise no more. Wheeler, however, emptied the balance of the sixteen shots into him, and then, reloaded his rifle and said: 'How do you like the way my gun shoots, old hoss? I'll bet my scalp against yours that you don't scalp any more white men in this canon very soon.' Bigfoot cried out in plain English, 'Don't shoot me anymore, you have killed me.' Wheeler walked up near the Indian, and, pulling out an ivory-handled revolver, gazed a moment at his fallen foe, then shouted out to me, 'Come down, whoever you are; there is no danger now.' I went to the spot and found Bigfoot bleeding from twelve wounds, both legs and one arm broken. The Indian asked for water, when Wheeler said, 'Hold on till I break the other arm; then I'll give you a drink.' Bigfoot said, 'Well, do it quick, and give me a drink and let me die.' Wheeler leveled his pistol, and at the report the arm fell useless to the ground. This to some may seem cruel, but I was yet afraid to go near this powerful and desperate savage monster. Wheeler went down to the creek, and brought up his canteen full of water, and placed it to the mouth of the Indian, who drank it all. Bigfoot then said he wished he had some whiskey, when Wheeler said he had a small bottle of whisky and ammonia, which he always carried in case of snake bites; that he could have it if he thought it would do him any good. Bigfoot said, 'Give it to me, quick; I'm getting blind.' Wheeler gave him a pint flask, filled with the strong fluid, mixed with a little water. The Indian drank it, every drop, and then said: 'I'm sick and blind,' and then fell back apparently dead.

After a few minutes he revived, and said that he was better, and that he wished us to to wash the dust and paint from his face, and see what a good looking man he was. We complied with his request, and, to our surprise, we found a fine-looking face, with the handsomest set of teeth we ever beheld. He had large, black, but wicked-looking eyes. His complexion had been almost white, but was now of course badly tanned. He had a heavy shock of long black hair, somewhat inclined to be kinky. He was of enormous size, and such hands, and especially feet, I never saw on any mortal before or since."[7]

Bigfoot continued to speak, it seems, on and on. He told of his early life; of all those who he had killed during his time in the Great Western Desert. This was no mere man - this Bigfoot. If even half of what he is supposed to have related were spoken aloud, as I have done a few times, it would take me some fifteen to twenty minutes, and that excludes the time it would have taken to drink a canteen full of water and a pint of "snakebite." Twelve rounds from a Henry rifle should have been enough to put down an elephant, let alone a human being, even such a human "monster" as our author would have us believe existed. And there are other thoughts that should concern those of us who dare to be rude pessimists as we hear the relation of Bigfoot's death. Wheeler supposedly pumped three rounds from an immensely powerful weapon into the body of our gigantic friend. Any one of those rounds packed enough "punch" to knock over a buffalo, let alone a human being, no matter what his size. Where did the first three rounds hit? In Bigfoot's fingers? Further, we are told that Wheeler poured a total of twelve of his sixteen rounds into our grand friend (fiend?). It would only have taken one well placed round to kill Bigfoot instantly. Wheeler must have either been one lousy shot, or one very nervous rifleman. And, as if these thoughts are not enough to convince the reader of the extreme problems associated with the narrative as told by Anderson, consider for a moment a few other thoughts...; What, in heavens name, was a knowledgeable pioneer like Anderson thinking of as he traveled across wilderness country, a country known to be infested not only with hostile Indians, but stage robbers and crooks of every stripe and kind, totally unarmed? This was not the way pioneers who traveled the wilderness trails of old Idaho Territory went in the 1860's. And what about Wheeler, if he even existed except in a fertile imagination; what was he doing at the pass where a stagecoach could be placed in jeopardy? Remember, if you will, that he was convicted of the robbery of a stage only months after his supposed killing of Bigfoot. Was he hiding out in wait for Bigfoot, or waiting for the chance to rob a stage? This is grand horse opera at its very best.

Finally, it is interesting to note that in the years 1866-67,

General George Crook of later Dakota and Arizona Indian fighting fame was in command of the Oregon and Idaho military command. He mentions many a hostile Indian in his reports, but never a Bigfoot, Nampa or Nampuh. In the Commissioner of Indian Affairs reports for the years 1866-67 and 1868, there are constant reports of battles, massacres, thefts and mayhem of every sort in the area where Bigfoot is claimed to have frequented, and yet, again, his name does not appear in the record. And none of the "pioneer" names that Anderson gives in his narrative turn up in the formal record either. Surprisingly, the official reports which formed much of the Commissioner of Indian Affairs documents are taken from local newspaper accounts.[8] Now, if newspaper accounts in the 1860's were as scurrilous as they are in this day and age, and I certainly expect they may have been even more so, then one may well wonder what really happened in those wild and wooly times.

How big was Bigfoot? Well, Anderson may have lost his horses, but he did manage to bring along his measuring tape. He recorded the following measurements for Bigfoot: "I had a tape line and rule in my pocket, with which I took the following exact measurements of this wonderful being: Around the chest, fifty-nine inches; height, six feet eight and a half inches; length of foot, seventeen and one half inches; around the ball of the foot, eighteen inches; around the widest part of the hand, eighteen inches. I am confident that he weighed at least 300 pounds, and all bone and sinew, not a pound of surplus flesh on him."[9] After Bigfoot was duly measured, he died peaceably. Wheeler and Anderson then tied ropes around the body and dragged it to the edge of the creek. They threw some brush and rocks on the corpse and buried Bigfoot and his broken gun in a shallow grave. Wheeler had promised Bigfoot as he lay dying that, if he told him all these wonderful particulars concerning his life, he would bury him so, not mutilate his body or take it to the fort. He "resolved" to say nothing of the affair, and thus the story did not come to first light until Anderson had it published in the *Idaho Statesman* of 1878.

In the *Idaho Statesman*, 1919 reprint of of the original story, there is even more sensationalism concerning poor Bigfoot. In an addition to the original is the following: "In the Statesman files of 1879 a sequel to the Bigfoot story is told, in itself most unusual if true. If any of the pioneers know of the present whereabouts of any of the petrified pieces of Bigfoot's body, particularly the last found eyeball, the pioneer editor would be glad to hear of it. It will be necessary to 'show her' before she will believe the story, which is as follows:

More of Bigfoot - It now appears that the remains of the big-footed fiend who was killed by Wheeler on Reynolds Creek in 1868 were completely petrified and then tumbled to pieces near the place where the body was hidden. Several fragments of different members of the body have been found, leaving only the left eyeball unaccounted for, and yesterday Joe Oldham, who has had Bigfoot on the brain ever since the story was published in the Statesman, succeeded in finding the missing eyeball among the archives of the sheriff's office. This orb of the Bigfoot optics is an elongated spheroid of a dark brown color, weighing about five pounds, and is encircled by a groove, making it appear as if it had been worn as an ornament by some inmate of the county jail. The iris and pupil of the eye have been well preserved in the process of petrification, and by looking closely through the pupil the images of Wheeler and Anderson can be distinctly seen through the crystallized, and now petrified lenses, painted in miniature on the retina. Mr. Oldham says he cannot account for the presence of this relic among the jewelry in his office, but thinks it was left there by Talton B. Scott, who was a guest of the institution for a short time."[10]

And, in a sense, the story of Bigfoot doesn't even end with this bit of hokum. In 1889, a small human figure, about one and one half inches in height, and supposedly representing a female figure was drawn from an artesian well sand-pump at Nampa, Idaho. It was retrieved from a depth of 320 feet, and initially, due to the depth from which it was retrieved, thought to share an age equivalent with that of Java Man. This strange object has been called the "Nampa Image."[11] So Bigfoot, or Nampa or Nampuh lives on in perpetuity.

Poor Bigfoot! In previous chapters, I have mentioned those who lived in the midst of the thunders. Bigfoot not only lived in the thunders, he was struck by a direct bolt of lightning!

NOTES

1. History of Idaho Territory Showing Its Resources and Advantages...,Wallace W. Elliot & Co., San Francisco, Calif., 1884. Reprinted edition of 400 bound copies, Ye Galleon Press, Fairfield, Wash., (1973).
2. Letter from Alan Virta, Head of Special Collections, Boise State University, dated September 18,1991.
3. Ibid note #1.
4. Ibid note #1.
5. Ibid note #1.
6. Ibid note #1.
7. Ibid note #1.
8. Message of the President of the United States and Accompanying Documents...Washington, 1867, and Report on Indian affairs by the Acting Commissioner for the year 1867. Washington, 1868.
9. Ibid note #1.
10. Newspaper - The Idaho Statesman, 1919, "Gruesome Story of Tragic Death of Indian Fiend," Ed. by Eva Hunt Dockery.
11. Hodge, Frederick Webb (ed.). Handbook of American Indians North of Mexico. Washington, GPO, 1910, Part 2, p. 18.

CHAPTER 7

THE LAST OF THE YOSEMITES

Her name was Maria Lebrado. At least that's what name was given to her by a foreign culture. Her tribal name was Totuya, translated into English as Foaming Water. She was the grand-daughter of the last great leader of the people we now call, the Yosemites - They cslled themselves Awani, a word which is thought to signify the Grizzly Bear.

The story of Maria, or Totuya, is a story of mans longstanding inhumanity to hid fellow man. It somehow seems to be a never ending story, and, personally, I find that very sad. At least when Original Peoples became involved in warfare, they fought their wars and once there was a victor, it was done with - but with other cultures it is different. These other cultures seem to have a penchant for wanting to continue to inflict pain and sorrow on the victims they have defeated. In the time in which I now live, I look, read and see in living color the horrors perpetuated by some of my fellow human beings, and I am depressed by all this. Even young people me talk to me and say they no longer want to read the newspapers or listen to the news on television. It is too distressing. Imagine then, if you will, the grand restorative power which the Original People have, that which enables them to look and see the Cain that dwells among us. Even so, people such as Totuya somehow found an inner peace or strength. She was caressed by the misty rains that follow the thunders.

YOSEMITE (AWANI)

This story of a woman who was among the very last of her people is perhaps more than just a story - it is a rediscovery of a human being and of a people. Maria Lebrado has, in this chapter, hopefully, been rescued from the ravages of time. In 1931 and 1932, her story was first told by a Mrs. H.J. Taylor (Rose Schuster)[1] in The University of California Chronicle. During that latter year the story was published in book form in San Francisco in what, I suspect, was a very limited edition. A copy of this scarce item came into my possession some ten years ago, and, as it had in the past, it simply gathered dust. Now, I think it is time that the dust and the cobwebs of the years are cleansed away and Maria Lebrado comes alive once more to remind us all of what might be considered our mortality.

Maria was more than just a "last survivor," of a doomed original people. She is just one of many who come from the past to haunt us for the sins of those who decimated the first peoples of California; and not only the first peoples of California, but all the first peoples who once inhabited this continent. Perhaps as Goldman and Leaky once conjectured, the first homo sapiens sapiens made their appearance in California, and the Garden of Eden did not have its place in some middle eastern country, but rather right under our very noses here on the North American continent.[2]

When one reads or otherwise hears about "Indian Wars," in this country, we hear much of the wars with the Iroquois of the New York area, the Shawnee, Miami, et al of Ohio and Indiana, the Ottawa, Chippewa and Potawatomi of the Great Lakes area, the Sioux of the northern plains, the Cheyenne of the middle plains, the Comanche, Apache, Blackfeet, Nez Perce and any lengthy list of peoples who fought their final battles in defense of their cultures, homes and ways of life. But, one never hears the names of California's peoples with perhaps only one exception, that being the Modoc of the northern part of the state. One reason which seems to account for this seeming lack of mention of California peoples involved in the "Indian Wars," can best be explained by mentioning one rather salient point concerning the peoples who inhabited our western shores. Anthropologists have been quick to tell us that the numerous peoples who inhabited the area we call California generally did not have tribal organization. Instead, they were loosely scattered throughout the coasts and the mountains in bands. They lived in a much ruder fashion then did most other Indian peoples on this continent - by ruder I mean they had only the most elementary types of shelters, and their livelihood was of a subsistence type. They were basic hunter-gatherers in a land which, at the time, had not the advantages of irrigation which would have allowed them to extend the reaches of their individual cultures. Language was yet another problem for the California peoples, as the diversity of languages was greater in the state then any other area on the continent.

   The Awani were a division of the Miwok who lived in Mariposa County. They sustained nine villages which contained only some 450 people when the first gold rush pioneers arrived in the area, although the population seems to have been larger at an earlier period of time.[3] With the news of gold and the advent of the '49ers, many of the indigenous cultures were placed in dire straits. The '49ers constituted a complete admixture of peoples from all areas of the country, but perhaps the greatest numbers of those who dared to dream the dream of striking it rich were drawn from the middle west. There were any number of young men who thought the life on the farm was just too dreary and unrewarding, and perhaps it really was that way. There were also the neer-do-wells who left the middle west perhaps just one step ahead of a sheriff or vigilance committee. They were, as are all people, good and bad. And as we see things today, it is always the bad who get the most press. I don't want to belabor the subject of the '49ers, except to point out that there are hundreds, perhaps thousands of journals still extant which were kept by these intrepid adventurers. Some simply told of the daily hardships that were endured, or else gave some brief treatises on the subject of mining per se, but there were some of these journals which told a different story. This was the shameful story - the story of the wanton destruction and removal of the original people. Bret Harte, I think, told in beautiful words the true life of these hardy '49ers, and in the same time era, Helen Hunt Jackson touched the American conscience with her writings. And, for my personal view, I think the story of Ishi, the last of the Mani people, who came forth from the wilderness in 1911, and whose story was so poignantly told by Theodora Kroeber in 1961 is the most sorrowful and yet the most touching. With this much said, I think we should now hear the story of Maria

Lebrado starting with the author's original preface.

"The story of To-tu-ya (Foaming Water) is one of interrupted childhood, unfulfilled longing, and silent suffering. She was born in Yosemite in the early eighteen forties. Ahwahnee was her playground; tumultuous Chorlock she loved; graceful, enchanting Pohono she feared. The monoliths - Tu-tock-ah-nu-la, Tis-sa-ack, To-ko-ya, Loya - given life in story by the Yosemite Indians, stood as protecting sentinels over her and her tribe. But scarcely a dozen years had passed when family and tribe were scattered by war and defeat at the hands of oncoming American miners.

While yet in her teens, she married a full-blooded Yosemite, a fellow refuge. Only the eldest of the five children she bore him survives. The untimely death of her husband brought added hardships. She married a Mexican miner, Lebrado Yerdies, whom she bore four daughters.

Life was nearing its close when To-tu-ya returned from exile to live a few days in her home of earliest memories. Souvenir-loving tourists came to look at her as she sat shelling a pile of acorns; one of them offered a nickle for an acorn from her hands. With deep feeling and resentment she pushed the coin aside and cried, 'No! Not five dollars one acorn, no! White man drive my people out-my Yosemite.'[4]

In her heart To-tu-ya treasured her Indian name, though the world called her Maria Lebrado. To-tu-ya-Foaming Water-will be heard as long as the melting snows pour in torrents over the granite walls of her childhood Yosemite."

This brief preface by Mrs. Taylor is just a prelude for a simple two chapter book. The first chapter, or part, is called, "The Return of the Last Survivor." I would be amiss if I did not record it in its entirety here complete with the footnotes which were appended to the original...

"Eight miles east of Mariposa, in the Mother Lode country of California, a trail leads over the hill from Dawson's Service Station to a little old log cabin. It was the home of Maria Lebrado,* granddaughter of Tenaya, chief of the Yosemite Indians. The gold rush brought conflict between miners and Indians, and in 1851 the Yosemites were driven by the Mariposa Battalion from their secluded home, their *Ahwahnee*.¥ At the point of the bayonet, about two hundred Indians, almost without clothing or food for the winter, made their way out by Inspiration Point and the Wawona road, or climbed the steep trail of Indian Canyon; among the latter was a girl named Maria, a girl of about ten years. Henceforth the Yosemite Indians were a scattered people, never to know the tie of band or tribe.

* Her Indian name was To-tu-ya (Foaming Water). The accompanying pictures were taken at Yosemite in July, 1929, at the time of her only visit to her birthplace.

¥ The Yosemite Indians called the valley 'Awani.' Interestingly, the name Yosemite was first applied to the Valley itself by Dr. Bunnel, a member of the battalion then in the very act of expelling the very people for whom he named it. 5

Seventy-eight years had passed when in July, 1929, Maria, then in her middle eighties, returned for the first time to the home of her childhood, her beloved *Ahwahnee.* The Kellogg and Golden Cup oaks produced abundantly that year, and Maria had gathered several bushels of their acorns. They lay in a large pile beside her tent in Indian Village, now inhabited mostly by Piutes and Monos. The horny outer shell of the acorns which had been cracked with stones, she removed with her hands. The soft brown inner covering was blown away when winnowed in her *chincoo* (basket shake). She pounded the acorns in a mortar with a stone pestle, leached out the tannin, and cooked the flour into a palatable mush. It was here in the Indian Village of Yosemite that I met Maria, last survivor of the exiled band, talked with her daily for a week as she prepared her acorn food, and heard from her lips an unwritten story.

Expulsion had left its impress on the child, and recollections of the event, though few, were vivid. There was the long climb through the snow, out of the Valley, over the mountains, in sorrow and humiliation. Then there was the figure of a soldier - 'Man with the red shirt....man with the red shirt,' she always replied to my questioning. And in these images is the essence of it all - the tragedy of a people filing out from their tribal home, forced out by the red-shirted Forty-niner!

But of the Valley itself and the life of her people memories were more numerous and varied. We went together to the cemetery. At the grave of Lucy, her cousin, she stood a moment in silence, then began to moan and wail loudly. Aside, her daughter explained, 'Indian do like that 'cause they Indian. We not tell Mamma now when relation die,'cause she not strong to cry three days and no sit, no eat.'

Moaning, Maria cried, 'All gone, long, long time 'go. I 'lone; no more Yosemite; long time 'go.' She stooped to pick some ferns near by and placed them on the grave. With hands extended, she chanted in strong, clear tones words that I did not understand, then turned to me and said in sympathetic voice, 'I Catholic - just little Catholic.' And she was comforted.

In the Indian room of the museum she looked about in wonderment. The 'long time 'go' became the present, and youth and joy and laughter returned to her. Her Indian words needed no interpreter, for the human face speaks a universal language. In basketry, she quickly detected whether made by Mono or Yosemite. A poorly made basket she pronounced 'too dirty,' pointing out where it lacked smoothness and form. She took a *hiki* (cradle), strapped the band across her forehead, and with delicious laughter walked about saying, 'Papoose, long time 'go.' The Indian arrowheads recalled the annual visit of the Monos into the Valley to trade their obsidian for acorns. Food was essential, likewise weapons. In awakened memories Maria lived over the distant past. Extending her arms to all that was about her she murmured, 'Long, long time 'go; I so big,' as she pointed to a little girl of about ten years.

Two young men drove us over the Valley she had not seen since her childhood. The wide open meadow, the Indian *Pantanko** of her day was covered with trees and shrubs. She shook her head, saying, 'Too dirty; too much bushy.' Everywhere, to her, the floor of the Valley seemed changed. She clasped her hands and exclaimed, 'All fixed up! Ahwahnee too dirty bushy; long time 'go big like all kick 'em.' We failed to understand. Loud and emphatically she repeated, 'Long 'go, pantanko big place like all kick 'em.' Still we did not grasp her meaning. She leaned forward, placed an imaginary ball and kicked it. 'Football field!' we exclaimed. Her laughter was delightful and unbounded. Later we came upon Leidig's Meadow, now the largest open space in the Valley. Her face beamed with joy as she cried, 'Pantanko! Ahwahnee!' The voice, the lights and shadows of the human face give expression beyond the power of words.

* Probably from the Spanish *fandango*, meaning 'dance,' but applied by Maria to the meadow where Indian festivals were held.

From the meadow she looked up at the rock walls of the Valley. The great monoliths stood unchanged. The waterfalls drawing their substance from the eternal source of rain and snow spoke to her as they had spoken in her childhood. Looking at Yosemite Falls she cried, 'Chorlock! Chorlock no gone!' She saluted Tu-tock-ah-nu-lah, now known as El Capitan. Her own Indian village had stood in full view of *Loya*, now Sentinel Rock. It seemed very dear to her. A momentary silence, then in quiet supplication she said,'Loya, Loya; long time 'go.' For us the wonders of Yosemite took on new and deeper meaning as the names so full of Indian lore fell from her lips. What loss to posterity and to history that these names have not been preserved. Bridal Veil, Vernal Falls, Mirror Lake, Sentinel Rock, Half Dome - these names are found throughout the world. Yosemite alone has a *Pohono*, a *Py-we-ack*, an *Ah-wi-yah*, a *Loya*, a *Tis-sa-ack*. In these names there is tradition and meaning that expresses the life of the people who originally possessed this Valley.

Maria's speech is laconic. Her words are Indian, Spanish, and English. It was expression rather than words that told her graphic story. pointing to Eagle Peak she told of gathering Indian potatoes along the slope and up the trail. I gave her the flower and bulb of the common brodiaea. Her face lit up with a smile. She bit into the bulb and laughed, saying, 'Walli, walli,' (i.e., from the earth).

Yosemite Valley is seven miles long and from a half-mile to a mile in width. Through its entire length flows the Merced River, on either side of which were located the Indian villages of her time. As we approached Bridal Veil Falls, Pohono (Spirit of the Evil Wind) in her day, Maria called sharply to the men, 'Boys, Pohono! Look out, boy! Pohono kill boy much.' We stopped. This, she told us was the western limit of the Indian wigwams, beyond which no Indian dared to build his *utcu* (house), for the evil wind swayed the falls. Indian names reveal the superstitions and imaginings of the Indian mind. When several Indians lost their lives in the stream that forms Pohono, it became bewitched. Anyone pointing his finger at Pohono, said Maria, would at once be killed by its poisonous spray. Bridal Veil stretches a rainbow across the Valley, and beyond it an Indian feared to go lest the evil spirit of Pohono claim him.

Though bent, Maria is physically strong. The gnarled hands, purple with age, speak clearly of a life of toil. Her shock of steel-gray hair is cut short. Her face is wrinkled with lines deep and innumerable, such as only time can trace through almost ninety summers of changing skies. Her mind is clear and alert; her senses are well preserved. Often as we shelled acorns together, we sat long without a spoken word; yet it was not an empty silence. The lights and shadows of the face may be read; they can never be translated into words.

I asked about the four sons. She looked afar off. The unshelled acorn fell from her fingers as she stretched forth her hand. Her body swayed. Her breath was a deep-drawn sigh. Slowly she whispered the names, 'Leandro, Cruz, Pietro, Angelo.' In the sacred silence I felt the agony and sorrow of the mother heart, the longing that time could not still. Almost breathlessly she repeated the names, and I, too, seemed to see them pass before me. In whispered tones I heard, 'Gone, all gone, long 'go.' Looking at me as if she had suddenly become aware of my presence, her face took on the look of revenge. In harsh and powerful tones she cried aloud, 'Gone! all gone, long 'go!' Each of the four sons had met a tragic death. We continued shelling acorns in silence. I asked about her daughters. She raised four fingers. 'Mary, full-blood!' she said with pride. Maria's first husband was a Yosemite. Her second husband was Mexican. With three fingers upraised she said, 'Andrea, Francisca, Grace,'* there was merriment in her eyes as she whispered in my ear, 'Half-breed.' Then followed roguish laughter.

* Candelaria, a fourth daughter by the Mexican husband, died in early womanhood.

The days were full for Maria, lone survivor of the Yosemite Indians who were driven from the Valley. Memory became a reality to her. Emotionally she lived over the tragic events of her life, events that have long since passed into cold, historical data; and to those who spent these days with Maria Lebrado, the facts of Yosemite's early history took on the life and atmosphere of human beings who suffered hopelessly.

We bade her good-bye. To the young men she curtsied as she said, 'Good-bye, boys; gracias, gracias.' Laying her hand on my shoulder, she said, 'Thank, thank; you white daughter.' Then she gave a high-pitched, piercing call that Tenaya gave when he summoned his people. The clear, strong, musical tones she trilled with long sustained breath that excited amazement. Maria stood beside her pile of acorns gazing at Tissa-ack, the cleft rock. Slowly the picture faded as we followed the winding road to Ahwahnee."[6]

Thus, we have now heard the story of Tatuya, she of the Foaming Waters. But, Maria Lebrado had little time left on this earth. The days of her many sorrows were coming to an end, and her biographer, the elusive Mrs. H.J. Taylor, nee Rose Schuster[7] would come again to Yosemite to visit with her mentor and, by now, dear friend. In the second part of her narrative is related, "The Death of the Last Survivor." Once it is re-recorded for posterity, it will be done...

"As flowers become few with the appearance of winter we see them as individuals. There is a love and tenderness for the last rose that no other can awaken; this one has gathered unto itself the beauty and fragrance and sadness of all its family. The lone tree, representative of a by-gone forest, stays the woodmans ax by the strength and power of its aloneness. The Indian band driven out of Yosemite Valley by the Mariposa Battalion in 1851 became intensely personified in Maria Lebrado, granddaughter of Tenaya, Chief of the Yosemites. As its last survivor she symbolized the history of her people. In her own lifetime she had experienced the tragic disintegration of the Yosemite tribe. Her death on April 20, 1931, broke our last link with Indian Yosemite.

Born in Yosemite about 1840, she knew the trails that led up the steep slopes to the hunting grounds of the Monos, with whom acorns were exchanged for obsidian to make arrowheads. She knew also the days of terror when the melodious call of Chief Tenaya assembling his people to feast of fandango was changed to the alarm call of threatening dangers. She knew the sorrow and humiliation of being driven out of her home, ever to be homeless and tribeless. She experienced the life of an exile. In the effort to maintain her tribe she bore a daughter and four sons by her Yosemite husband. The husband and the four sons died. She married a Mexican miner and bore four daughters. She yet felt the pride of tribal blood; these, her later children, were 'not Yosemites,' she said, adding humorously, - 'half-breeds.'

After 78 years of hardship and suffering, sorrow and anguish, Maria, a woman of nearly ninety years, visited the Yosemite Valley in July, 1929. That she was a distinguished guest moved her not. Dignified in bearing, she revealed strength and courage rather than years. Standing with arms folded she looked a statue and her silence was ominous. Her well-kept shock of steel-gray hair that once hung in thick black braids to her knees had for many years been cut. This was an outward expression of sorrow for the four sons who met tragic deaths. One looked at her time-worn face and words were lost in reflection. Deep experiences had left their traces, yet she had not lost the memory of joyous years. She still retained delicious laughter and a quick sense of humor. Deep in her breast was a heart of love that gave itself in true friendship.

In response to a message, I visited her in the summer of 1930 and again in the early autumn. Her look, her touch, her voice, were full of unuttered expression. She took from my arms a little child and held it to her breast saying, 'Baby, baby,' then in a low, sad voice she whispered, 'All gone, long, long 'go, my all gone.' I wanted to hear once more Tenaya's call as he summoned his people. Extending her hands and lifting her head she gave in clear, musical notes a call that vibrated in the surrounding hills. The marvel was her sustained breath. A moment of silence and she repeated the beautiful call. Never again shall I hear that music. The memory of it lures me to the freedom and naturalness and charm of Indian life that understands the streams and rocks and skies.

Early spring in 1931 brought word of Maria's illness. It was late afternoon when we arrived at her cabin on Bear Creek. The sun no longer shone and clouds were lowering. Surprised and overjoyed at our coming she stroked my arm with her feeble, bony hand, saying, 'White daughter come far, far see me.' She motioned to the blanket wrapped about her. I had given it. Then she laid her hand over her heart, then over mine. I sat in silence by the bedside of my friend.

I spent the night with my Indian friends. The Indian welcome, 'This house is yours,' invites refreshing rest. The clouds dropped their rain; the sun shone on a new day. Maria seemed stronger. Taking leave she clasped my hand in both of hers. 'Gracias, gracias, you come far, far. Thank, thank. I sick. I go.' She pointed upward, then moved her hand over her body and said, 'Graveyard.'

Five weeks later, on April 21, I received a telegram announcing her death. A few hours later another telegram informed me that the funeral would be at ten o'clock Wednesday morning. we left at once by auto, spending the night en route. With an early start and good roads we soon reached Myers, eights miles east of Mariposa. There we left the highway and for a mile or more followed a 'through-cut,' rough and winding, that leads up Cocyade Gulch and Bear Creek to Maria's cabin, and arrived shortly after eight o'clock Wednesday morning. From within came rhythmic wailing moans of relatives paying tribute to one they loved.

We entered. The body of Maria lay on a white covered board. The daughters alone had closed her eyes, folded her hands, and clothed her body for burial. My childhood conception of a princess lay before me. She wore a black silk dress. Over the knees and reaching to the feet lay a beautiful piece of bright pink satin. A similar piece, green in color, covered the body. The sleeves were ornamented at the wrists with beaded bands. A beaded belt, the gift of her daughter, lay diagonally across her breast. A beaded headband, such as Indian hands alone can make, lay across her forehead. The canvas-covered casket stood beside the body. Ten o'clock proved too early for the funeral. 'Two o'clock,' some thought, 'would be better.' Others said, 'Perhaps three o'clock.' Another said that 'At four o'clock surely all who were coming would be there.' And so it was held at four o'clock.

Maria had requested an Indian funeral such as so often she had given to others. 'White people do White funeral, Indian like Indian funeral,' she had told her daughters. So the funeral dance of Tenaya's day - a custom unused for many years - was decided upon.

The granddaughter of Chief Tenaya was no ordinary Indian. His blood flowed in her veins. At his funeral, in 1853, with unceasing wail and dance, she paid him tribute for three days and all these days she touched no food. His sons had been killed, and with their death she had become the embodiment of her people. Maria was a medicine woman. She had diagnosed and cured many ills. Her funeral must not be wanting in tribute due her rank.

The tom-toms played. For more than an hour relatives and friends joined in the song and dance as they circled about Maria. As four o'clock neared, the body was placed in the casket. The green veil lying at the head was spread over Maria's face. With heartfelt cries the daughters placed one last kiss and said their last good-bye. The casket was closed. Four young Indians, grandsons and relatives, with four other young Indians beside them, took up the casket and led the procession of one hundred and twenty-five up the winding trail for half a mile or more. The cemetery is on a hill-top which commands a view of mountain meadows, deep canyons and distant ranges.

The grave was lined with white muslin and covered with fronds of woodwardia. Here and there a flower added a touch of color. The casket was placed. Five or six Indian youths stood beside the grave and sang, swaying as they measured time. At the foot of the grave stood half a dozen women interpreting the singing with outstretched and uplifted arms. As the casket was lowered, 'earth to earth,' was said. The last distressing cries of the younger daughters were heard. Mary - Yosemite and Maria's firstborn - stood apart with head erect, shoulders back, and arms folded. every muscle of her face was fixed. Her eyes were partly closed. the universal event of death had no terror for her. There was courage and understanding and triumph in that statue. She stood as the interpretation of Browning's Prospice.

In the grave were placed things dear to Maria. First a woolen blanket. An Indian youth went into the grave and spread it smoothly over the casket. All through her illness it had been wrapped about her. It touched me deeply, for it was the one I had given her. A blanket of Indian design she had used and treasured for many years was also placed on the casket. The grave was filled. The flowers were placed upon the mound. The wreath we had made of blue and golden brodiaea we laid at the head of the grave of this native daughter. The slanting rays of the sun shone warm and bright on the last survivor's grave.

We possess her Yosemite. She sleeps in a lonely and unknown spot. Time may place a tablet on this grave. Pilgrims may wear an everlasting trail to the hilltop - a belated tribute for the suffering and exile inflicted upon her."

Thus ends the story of the last of the Yosemites. Maria Lebrado rests in silence - to the outside world, she is an unknown. Perhaps she now knows no more pain, and the gentle rains have, these many years, refreshed her soul.

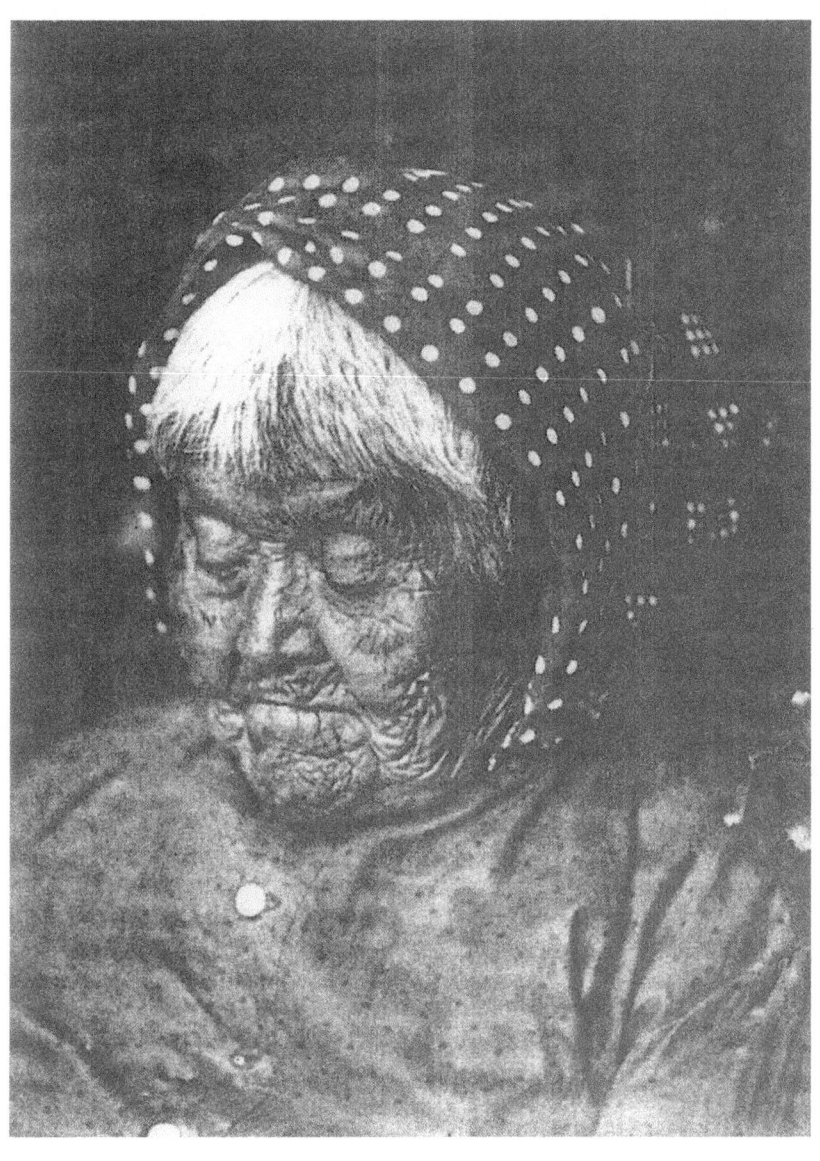

Totuya (Foaming Water) A.K.A. Maria LeBrado

NOTES

1. Letter from reference librarian, David Decklebaum, of the University of California, Los Angeles, dated 10 October, 1991.
2. Goodman, A. American Genesis. N.Y., (1979).
3. Hodge, Frederick Webb (ed.). Handbook of American Indians North of Mexico. Washington, GPO, 1907 and 1910 (in two parts).
4. Taylor, Mrs. H.J. The Last Survivor. Johnck & Seeger, San Francisco, 1932.
5. Ibid note # 3, Part 1, p. 118. "Powers states that the name Yosemite is a distorted form of the Miwak *uzumaite*, 'grizzly bear....,' " Awani was the name given to the valley by the Indians themselves.
6. Ibid note # 4.
7. Ibid note # 1 - The UCLA archives has no publishing history whatsoever concerning Mrs. Taylor.
8. Ibid note # 4.

CHAPTER 8

PROPHET OF DISASTER

In this chapter, I will attempt to analyze the life and history of a man named Wabokishiek (White Cloud). I will also attempt to analyze some of the descendants of this prophet. Wabokishiek was among the leading spirits in the so-called Black Hawk War in Illinois in 1832. The terrible finale of this stain upon the land ended at a place where the Bad Axe river flows into the Mississippi from the state of Wisconsin.

This is also the story of the descendants of Wabokishiek. It is, in a sense, more than just one story, In certain respects, it is is a story of the ancestors, of those who came before, but it is more then that - It is a blending, an amalgam of past and present. It is also a story of a friend of this day and age, a proud legacy from the past and of a family which grows and prospers both spiritually and materially in both the old and the new ways.

It is, lastly, a connected series of stories which will bring the generations into focus.

Meet out thunder people if you will - Wabokishiek (White Cloud), Wahquahboshkuk (Fish in Roiled Water), and Shau-nos-ka (First Lightning from the South).

WINNEBAGO-SAC

For this writer, the story of Wabokishiek (White Cloud) began with a chance meeting with his great grandson, Shau-nosh-ska (First Lightning in the South). Shau-nosh-ska and I first met in the spring of 1988. He was an honorary visitor to St. Charles, Illinois on the occasion of the unveiling of a bronze statue in honor of the Potawatomi Nation. He was presently Chairman of the Prairie Band of the Potawatomi Nation whose reserve is located at Mayetta, Kansas. Our meeting was somewhat brief, but as we began to converse, he made a comment to me to the effect that his grandfather fought in the last battle of the plains of Kansas during the 1840's. Being sensible to a cultural politeness towards the Potawatomi people, I didn't press Shau-nosh-ska with questions at the time. However, I did ask him if someday he would tell me the story of his ancestor. Sure enough, a few weeks later, a letter arrived from his western home. In it was the story of his ancestor's grand battle. According to my new found friend, his grandfather was with a hunting party on the plains of Kansas sometime in the 1840's, when the party were met by a band of Pawnee, and somehow a battle took place. The story as related by Shau-nosh-ska, (Christian name George L. Wahquahboshkuk), is from his hand, as follows:

"After the Pawnee raided a Potawatomi village, a War party was sent out, my grandfather was in the party when the Prairie Band Potawatomi caught up to the raiding party (in western Kansas). A battle ensued until one last warrior was left and my grandfather was battling him. The Potawatomi warriors sat upon their mounts as they stood on a creek bank, cheering for young Wabokishiek. It is said the fight lasted a long time (some say half-a-day). 'He dirtied up the water as he fought.' It may have been, he was quite young, being the reason they fought so long.

The account goes on, that during the fight, they would disappear under the water for lengths at a time, finally my grandfather came up by himself, a survivor..."[1]

As the stream in which the battle took place had become badly muddied up from the turmoil of the battle, the victor was given a warrior name by his fellow Potawatomi, Sac, Kansa and Kickapoo. He was, from that day forward called "Wahquahboshkuk," (Fish in Roiled [or Muddied] Water). He would no longer be known as Wabzhick in the Potawatomi villages. George wrote me that he truly believed that the battle may have gone on for half-a-day day, as he himself had seen combat in Viet Nam, and mentioned to me that he himself had been in battles in that far distant land in which time was forgotten in the heat of battle. Well, thought I, this is a grand story - quite interesting, but I wondered, other than George's story, if there were any historical documentation for this affair. Only by chance, a few weeks after receiving the letter from my friend, I just happened to locate the historical document which told the entire story of Wahquahboshkuk's battle.[2]

" ...an incident which occurred in July, 1848, had sent them (the Potawatomi) flying in panic to the south side of the river. A small party of Potawatomi of the family of Paid, together with a handful of Kickapoo and Sauk, had gone out west of the reserve to hunt buffalo. On the way the hunters fell in with the main body of the Kansa Indians, who were also in search of the same game, and smoked with them a friendly pipe of peace. Meanwhile a band of Pawnee came up to the four allied camps, but deterred presumably by the rather formidable strength of the latter from making an attack, they sent a messenger to the Potawatomi and their friends with pledges of good will and an invitation to join them on the hunt. The messenger was well received and dismissed in peace, but on his way back was fired upon and killed by a Kansa Indian. Enraged by the murder, the Pawnee attacked the four camps. In the engagement that ensued five Pawnee were killed and their scalps carried off by the Potawatomi and Kickapoo..." The leader of the Potawatomi party in this fray was a man called Kack-kack (The Duck Hawk). Kack-kack was a respected leader of the Prairie Band of the Potawatomi Nation for a great many years. He died at the reputed age of eighty eight at his home on February 16, 1907.[3,4]

Upon locating this bit of information, I wrote to George with a photocopy of the entire original. He soon wrote back, and told me how pleased he was that I was able to confirm the story of his ancestor. Now, in the story quoted above there is no mention of the individual Potawatomi/Pawnee battle in the creek bed, but George assures me that this is the battle in which this event occurred. And then, he gave me a rather grand surprise - something that had I asked about (impolitely in Potawatomi culture), I would otherwise never have been told. This brave Potawatomi warrior, Wahquahboshkuk, was a son of the noted Winnebago-Sac prophet, Wabokishiek. Now, for historians in Illinois, Iowa and Wisconsin who have studied that stain upon the land which has been called the Black Hawk War, Wabokishiek is very important. He was one of the major players in this terrible drama in 1832. By most who knew him before or at the time, he was simply called, "The Prophet." He was despised by many, if not most, of the frontiersmen and pioneers of the period, but like others who were caught up in the "thunderstorms" of racial hatred, he was simply a victim. The record of his life, what is known of it, tells of a very different person then the bloodthirsty, evil savage he was reputed to be. Among the many sad, unfounded and prejudicial statements made concerning the Prophet are the following:[5]

In speaking of the receipt of a portrait of the Prophet received by the Wisconsin State Historical Society in 1855 is this comment - "The countenance of the Prophet indicates a malignant leer, which, with his dark massive locks, is in perfect keeping with his character....," and again, " We also learned that the Sauks and Foxes had been instigated to their present course by Waw-be-ka-shick, the Prophet, a half Winnebago and half Sauk, and possessing much influence with both nations from his assumption of the sacred character, from his talents, his inveterate hostility to the Americans, and his cold-blooded cruelty."[6] And, the most venomous of all the commentaries I have seen; " White Cloud, the prophet, was Black Hawk's evil genius. He was a shrewd, crafty Indian, half Winnebago and half Sac, possessing much influence over both nations from his assumption of sacred talents . . . . He had many traits of character similar to those possessed by Tecumseh's brother, but in a less degree. His hatred of the whites was inveterate; he appears to have been devoid of humane sentiments; he had a reckless disposition, and seemed to enjoy sowing the seeds of disorder for the simple pleasure of witnessing a border chaos. He was about forty years of age when his sinister agitation bore fruit; was nearly six feet in height, stout and athletic; had a large, broad face; a short, blunt nose; full eyes, large mouth, thick lips, a full head of shaggy hair, and his general appearance indicated deliberate, self-contented savagery."[7] Wow! This final statement that I have quoted is a masterpiece of slanted hate literature. There is not one statement made to corroborate any of the innuendos or direct accusations regarding the Prophet's real character. Even the noted artist George Catlin commented rather nastily concerning the

Prophet; "The Prophet... is about forty years old and nearly six feet high, stout and athletic...the priest of assassination or secret murder."[8] Of course, this author must admit that he has never thought that George Catlin was much of an artist per se; he just managed to be first on the spot whenever history was being made. As a realist, in artistic terms, he left much to be desired. But, I lead myself into fields far astray with these comments. I think it best, at this point in my narrative, to look strongly at the *real* Prophet and to attempt to give the reader a better perspective on the man.

    Wabokishiek was born about 1794 at a village about thirty five miles above the mouth of the Rock River where it debouches into the Mississippi River. There is presently a town named in his honor called Prophetstown, Illinois in Whiteside county at the spot, and the village site is presently set aside as a park. Wabokishiek's father was a Sac by the name of Waunoshick and his mother was a Winnebago of the family of Broken Arm.[9] It is not known for certainty if Wabokishiek participated in the War of 1812; if so he would have been a young warrior of approximately eighteen years of age; a good age for an Indian fighting warrior in those days. Black Hawk, his friend and confidant is known to have figured in that war, and the presence of Wabokishiek with his friend and possible relation[10] would not have been surprising.

    Of his life during the early part of the 1800's, we known practically nothing. In the year 1829, Caleb Atwater of Ohio visited at the Prophet's village. His report of that same year was highly inflammatory. "His two or three hundred followers were a variegated rabble of little use in either peace or war consisting, for the most part, consisting of outcasts and invalids from other tribes."[11] Atwater further characterized the people that lived at the Prophet's village as "deformed or dwarfs, a nightmarish aggregation adhering to the prophet because they were unwelcome anywhere else." Atwater did not realize what he had written concerning the Prophet. What he really characterized was not a "prophet," as such, but a spiritual. And for those who are unacquainted with the original people concept of a "spiritual," I will attempt to give some brief thought as to what such a personage was expected to be. He was not a "prophet," in our sense of the word. He was a man or a woman who simply was a very religious person, (if such a term I might be permitted to use); a person who was recognized as having a special relationship with not only the Great Spirit,

Wabokishiek (White Cloud) - The Prophet

Portrait by George Catlin from *Letters & Notes* .., Tosswill and Myers, 1841. Author's Private Collection.

but one who both lived and acted in a sacred manner for the best interests of the generality of the people among whom they lived. Thus, Caleb Atwater, when he attempted to denigrate Wabokishiek because of the people who had flocked to his standard, really showed the true character of the man. If, indeed, Wabokishiek's village consisted of outcasts, i.e., people deformed or dwarfs," then the true spiritual personage of White Cloud is easily understood. Unknowingly, Atwater, in making what he thought were comments intended to inflame, instead showed a man who cared; a man who cared for the least of all his people. It is probably true that White Cloud used all the wiles at his command in order to bring a kind of special and mystical aura to those unfortunates who came to his village for both physical and spiritual assistance. Atwater speaks not of a "prophet," but of a saint. A saint? Who would dare call Wabokishiek a saint? Alas, in His time, who would have called Jesus Christ anything other then a blasphemer? To the historian, the anthropologist or the ethnohistorian, such talk is probably - no, surely - heresy. Many years ago, I was given a series of "definitions" by Indian friends. One was the definition of a "religious; the other was the definition of a "spiritual." At the time, I swore to keep these original people definitions, if such they can be called, confidential. To this day, that is the case. Notably, I hear and see in these days that many of our "experts" who claim to have knowledge of world religions and/or concepts, referring to the beliefs of various cultures as "myth." Now, the word "myth" has a connotation far different from that which forms the basis for the beliefs of indigenous peoples throughout this wide world of ours.

    To every group of people who have religious/spiritual beliefs, these tenets or dogmas are far from being anything called "myths." Myth refers to fictitious stories or stories of dubious import or magic. To true believers, whatever their belief, no stories within the confines of their dogma are myths. This is what is called faith. They are the unabsolved, pure truth, and, the truth, whatever that may be, is strangely similar in all the major religions; and that includes Original People religions.

    For the present, let us reserve our judgement a while and hear more concerning White Cloud. What occurred within the confines of his village may forever be a mystery, but his actions, as recorded by those who had occasion to know or meet him intimately, tell of a far different person then what we have heard of so far. From the pen of   Major Thomas

Forsyth, Indian trader for many years among the Sac and Fox, and Indian Agent at Peoria, Illinois, we have the following: "Many a good meal has the Prophet given to people traveling past his village, and very many stray horses has he recovered from the Indians, and restored to their rightful owners, without asking any recompense whatsoever."[12]

During the time just prior to the Black Hawk War, Colonel Gratiot, the Indian agent for the Winnebago visited at the village of Wabokishiek. Gratiot was considered humane among the Indian peoples and was thought most able to influence the Prophet and his people to turn back Black Hawk's "British Band" to Iowa. Upon entering the village of the prophet, Gratiot and his party were surrounded by the hostiles and taken prisoner. He was taken to the wigwam where the Prophet lived and allowed to explain the object of his visit, but was unable to persuade the Indians from their course. The warriors from the British Band, along with some disaffected Potawatomi and a number of Kickapoo, called out for the death of Gratiot and his party. But Wabokishiek was too much of a man to allow these emissaries to be killed, and after a few days he found an opportunity to allow the party to escape.[13] This certainly does not sound like the blood-thirsty savage or assassination of murder.

As a matter of fact, the action of Wabokishiek, in allowing the Gratiot party to escape, may very well explain his actions throughout the Black Hawk War. Neither Black Hawk or Wabokishiek intended offensive war. What they intended was to assert, what they considered their rights to live as free men in their own homes. If they could not do that, they would travel northward to the country of the Winnebago, and if necessary even to Canada. The Treaty of 1804, which was signed at St. Louis, and well oiled with "demon rum," was the vehicle which ultimately forced the Sac and Fox from Illinois. The land of the Sac and Fox was henceforth (after the war of 1812), called the military bounty land, as it was to be reserved for veterans of that conflict. Very few veterans actually took the land, instead many of them sold their rights to the area. Soon an unscrupulous rabble entered into the country, and surprisingly, the Sac and Fox managed to remain at peace with these interlopers. A second treaty in 1816 confirmed the first treaty, and this treaty was signed by Black Hawk, although he later complained bitterly that he did not understand, that by signing the treaty, he was signing away the village of his birth.

The status quo was maintained for a number of years, until early in 1832. White squatters had built cabins and grog shops right in the midst of Black Hawk's village. The old warrior still kept the peace, but relations between the whiskey peddlers, land hungry settlers, assorted rabble and the Indians became severely strained. Black Hawk was warned to leave the land or else... He signed a treaty at Rock Island that same year and removed to the Iowa side of the river. But, in the meantime, he had sent his first war leader, Napope (Soup) to visit with their old British allies in Canada. Napope returned to tell Black Hawk that their former British allies were ready and willing to help the Sac and Fox to assert their rights. Now, this talk by Napope was all that was needed to spur on Black Hawk. Whether or not Napope ever heard such talk from the British at Manitoulin Island is doubtful. The question is whether he simply lied in order to obtain some action among his companions, or totally misunderstood the words that were told him may never be known. Very shortly, in early April, 1832, Black Hawk with some five hundred fighting men and another five hundred non-combatents crossed the Mississippi River at the Yellow Banks (now Oquawka, Illinois). The entire crossing and march northward was entirely peaceful, yet Governor Ninian Edwards felt compelled to call out the state militia. The Prophet had invited Black Hawk and his followers to come to his village just up the Rock River. And, as if to make his point, on April 5th, Wabokishiek went voluntarily to the Sac agent's house at Rock Island. He revealed to the agent Felix St. Vrain, that he had invited the band to join him at his village. St. Vrain was astonished at the admission, and pointed out that such a visit was a direct violation of the articles of the treaty which had been signed the previous summer. The Prophet expressed ignorance of the articles and added that had he known of them, he would not have extended the invitation. The next morning, the Prophet met with Major Bliss, commander of the garrison at Rock Island. In response to questions from Bliss, the Prophet remarked that he saw nothing wrong with joining his village with that of Black Hawk's. They had no intention of returning to Black Hawk's village (Saukenuk), and they were dissatisfied with the new lands in Iowa. When Major Bliss warned Wabokishiek that, if Black Hawk were to cross the river there would be war, the Prophet turned on his heel and stalked out of the meeting room. One of his followers said, "He was very angry."[14]

Black Hawk and his British Band, after spending a few scant days at the village of the Prophet, and trying, for the most part, unsuccessfully, to get the Potawatomi to side with them in their grievances, the now unified band began a leisurely trek towards the north-northeast. Little did they realize, that a drunken rabble was making haste to overtake them. This was the Illinois militia battalion under the command of Isaiah Stillman. At the town now named after the man and the event - Stillmans Run - the two hundred eighty some odd volunteers caught up with the rear guard of Black Hawk's band. Instead of offering battle, Black Hawk, instead offered a flag of truce. His messengers were brutally shot down, and in the murky dimness of the forests at twilight, the war whoop rent the air. Rifle balls tore through the lower canopy of the forest, and also through the bodies of twelve of Stillman's men. With an incredibly small rear guard force of only forty warriors, Black Hawk caused Stillman's entire command to flee the field in utter disarray. But, what must have seemed like such a simple battle, was, in reality, the beginning of the end for Black Hawk, White Cloud, the Soup and their followers. Of the one thousand plus human beings who started on this journey for freedom, only one hundred plus lived to the end. Black Hawk and White Cloud and their sons and families lived through the ordeal, but were captured by the Winnebago and brought to Prairie du Chien, Wisconsin. The Prophet was imprisoned first at Jefferson Barracks in St. Louis, and later at Fortress Monroe. The Prophet's brother, who was named Ottako or Atako,[15] was also imprisoned with him. The youngest son of White Cloud was released from captivity due to his young age. This was the son who later became Wahquahboshkuk. He had taken the same name of his father. In 1832, he would have been approximately six or seven years of age.[16] There were two other known sons. One was known by the name of Sozsha, who was a half brother, and there was an adopted son named Pawushut[17] who remained with his father in his captivity. Pawushut appears to have been a young man in 1832, perhaps in his late teens or early twenties. The Prophet and his adopted son were released from captivity at Prairie du Chien, Wisconsin a few days prior to August 3, 1833. White Cloud eventually went to live among the Sac in Iowa in obscurity, until their removal to Kansas, and died among the Winnebago in 1841.[18]

It was now the era of the young White Cloud. He was, as

mentioned earlier, given the warrior name, Wahquahboshkuk in 1848. Now, in modern day Potawatomi orthography, it would be spelled as Wakwaboshkah. However, the old spelling is maintained in this day. Besides proving himself a valiant warrior on the plains, our Wahquahboshkuk proved himself in various other ways. It is almost assured that he was formally adopted by the Prairie Band Potawatomi. This is evinced by the clan name (Shau-nosh-ska) which his grandson bears. As Wahquahboshkuk matured in years, he became an active leader among his adoptive Potawatomi brothers and sisters. He was politically active in negotiating a removal to northern Wisconsin based on the 1861 Potawatomi Treaty.19 His efforts stalled back in the 1860's, and I am sure that he would be proud to know that his grandson George continues to attempt to complete the process today. But Wahquahboshkuk had much more work to do for his people, and indeed all Original peoples. In 1887 the Dawes Act became the law of the land. The Dawes Act attempted to do away with land in common status for all Indian nations and tribal groups in the United States. For the beleaguered Original peoples, this act was tantamount to losing all vestiges of culture, of family, religion, of all the ties which made the Original people unique among human beings. Land was to be allotted to individuals; individuals who had not yet even been accepted as citizens in their own land. It was not until 1924 that "American Indians" gained the rights of citizenship. The Prairie Band, under the strong influence of Wahquahboshkuk, were quick to fight back against this injustice as did other tribal groups throughout the United States. This was a time of supposed acculturation; a time when Indian children were taken into Indian boarding schools; a time when the children were not allowed to speak their own language without fear of severe punishment. This was the start of an experiment, possibly well intended in the minds of late Victorians, to take the Indian into the great "melting pot," the so-called mainstream of white society. This was also the time when so much of the original oral histories of Original people cultures was lost forever. From the Euro-American viewpoint, this was perhaps a way of salving the conscience - a way of eradicating the past forever. But thanks to men such as Wahquahboshkuk, the plan was doomed to failure. In 1891, the Presidential order to implement the allotment of the reservation in Kansas was received. Wahquahboshkuk obtained assistance in his battle against the

Federal bureaucracy from unusual quarters. Nsowakwet, a Potawatomi from north central Wisconsin and Tom Topash from the Michigan Potawatomi soon appeared on the reservation and acted as allies in the fray. Thus, the Prairie Band now had organized opposition to the Government and their corrupt agents. Delegations soon deluged Washington and they were assisted by other Original people delegations in their efforts. Wahquahboshkuk and his assistant Nibakwa (He Walks at Night) were appointed members of the warrior society. Wahquahboshkuk acted strongly partly due to the fact that he was a literate man. He constantly signed his numerous letters and correspondence under the nom de paix, "The Gentil Brave."[21] Although he called himself "gentil," this aging warrior was anything but peaceable. He was ready and able for a fight with the powers to be at all times. Although he was considered a somewhat benign man, and a photograph of him at the time makes him look rather innocuous, Wahquahboshkuk was, in reality, a very powerful and charismatic person. Roily Water proved to be a warrior - no - a wkama (leader) with persuasions from what might be called the old ways. In 1891,

 Wahquahboshkuk and Agent Scott had their first major confrontation. Scott called for a contingent of the Seventh Cavalry (a Seventh Cavalry who later that same year would commit one of the great atrocities in American history, the slaughter at Wounded Knee, South Dakota). Upon the arrival of the army, Wahquahboshkuk and Scott entered into a ferocious argument. For his part, Wahquahboshkuk and his right hand man Nibakwa placed themselves between the Seventh Cavalry and the disaffected Indians. Here was the old warrior, not fighting in the bed of a creek, but boldly standing forth on the open prairie to defend the people and the way of life that he loved. Like his father, Wabokishiek, before him, he showed himself a worthy and brave man, ever ready to defend those who could not defend themselves. Surprisingly, the Seventh Cavalry (Custer's old regiment) didn't kill the Fish in Roiled Water or the Man Who Walks at Night. But, in August, Agent Scott got his revenge. Wahquahboshkuk was arrested by Colonel Forsyth of the Seventh Cavalry. To the everlasting credit of the people of Kansas, and particularly of the city of Topeka, there were citizens who saw the arrest of the grand old man of the Potawatomi as having his civil rights violated. In December, 1891, Wahquahboshkuk and Nibakwa hired an attorney and had habeus corpus proceedings filed in a Topeka court. They further advanced their case the next spring by filing a civil suit for damages of $11,000 each against agent Scott.22 When all else failed, agent Scott had the two "offenders remanded to the stockade at Fort Riley, Kansas. But, seven months later they were released and promptly returned to the reservation and continued their efforts to continue to undermine the allotment act. Scott claimed a victory, but, the reality of the situation was that the agent had been badly bested by Roily Water and He Walks at Night. In 1892 the "Gentil Warrior" and his followers started to make regular visits to Washington and by various stratagems, by 1894, agent Scott was forced to tender his resignation from his post. The agent who took Scott's place, L. F. Pearson fared no better then his predecessor. In 1895, he too was gone and he was succeeded by George W. James. James ended the century by allowing a small, but elite group of Potawatomi to handle affairs on the reservation, and although the Potawatomi people were in dire straits, they somehow managed to struggle through this time of difficulty. And thus the Potawatomi, and Wahquahboshkuk, struggled into the twentieth century, poor, dispirited, but still clinging to what little was still left of the old ways.

In 1893, in the midst of all this turmoil, Wahquahboshkuk bore a son. He was named Levi. Levi claimed that he was born in 1893, but according to his son, I have this brief and somewhat humorous story: "Bear in mind that, in those days, birth records for Indians were unheard of. So when they say my grandfather was born in the 1830's, they could be off ten years or more. As with my dad Levi Wahquahboshkuk, he had no birth certificate. He told everyone he was born in 1893, but when he had a physical examination the doctor told him he was at least twenty years older than he was telling everyone (He really got upset with the doctor).23

Now, there is my brother George. He has six children who will follow in his ways, and hopefully in the ways of his forefathers. George is a grand person. He is my brother/friend, and personally, I see a great physical resemblance between him and his great grandfather Wabokishiek. George is perhaps no prophet, but he is much more, he is a man - and he is, above all, a friend and a survivor. His people are those who have entered into the turmoil of the thunders and have been washed clean by the rains. These are our Original People.

Kche Migwetch (Many thanks)

NOTES

1. Letter from George Wahquahboshkuk dated October 5, 1988.
2. Garraghan, Gilbert J., S.J. The Jesuits of the Middle United States. Chicago, 1984 - reprint of the 1938 edition in three volumes.
3. Records Commissioner of Indian Affairs. Washington, GPO, 1848.
4. Kansas Historical Society Records.
5. Collections of the State Historical Society of Wisconsin. Volume I, Madison, 1903 (Reprint edition), "Whittelesey's Recollections," p.72.
6. Collections of the State Historical Society of Wisconsin. Volume X, Madison, 1888, "Indian Campaign of 1832," p.155.
7. Collections of the State Historical Society of Wisconsin. Volume XII, Madison, 1892, "The Black Hawk War of 1832," p. 224.
8. McCracken, Harold. George Catlin and the Old Frontier. New York, (1959).
9. Letter of Samuel C. Stambaugh to Winfield Scott, Prairie du Chien, August 13, 1832, photocopy in author's collection.
10. Callender, Charles in Handbook of North American Indians. Smithsonian Institution, Washington, 1978. Volume 10, "Sauk."
11. Eby, Cecil. That Disgraceful Affair the Black Hawk War. New York, (1973).
12. Kinzie, Mrs. John H. Wau-bun the Early Day in the North-West. New York, 1856.
13. Hodge, Frederick Webb (ed.). Handbook of American Indians North of Mexico. Washington, GPO, Part 2, 1910.
14. Whitney. Ellen M. (ed. & comp.). Collections of the Illinois Historical Society. Springfield, 1973. Volume II in the series (Volume XXXVI), p. 230.
15. ----------------------- Collections of the Illinois Historical Society. Springfield, 1973. Volume II in the series (Volume XXXVI), p. 165, note # 2.
16. Ibid note # 1.
17. Whitney, Ellen M. (ed. & comp.). Collections of the Illinois Historical Society. Springfield, 1973. Volume II in the series (Volume XXXVI), p. 1189, note # 1.
18. Ibid note # 13.
19. Sixtieth Congress, Session II, Ch. 263, 1909.
20. Letter from George L. Wahquahboshkuk dated February 24, 1992.
21. Clifton, James A. The Prairie People Continuity and Change in Potawatomi Culture 1665-1965. Regents Press, University of Kansas, (1977).
22. Ibid note # 21.
23. Ibid note # 1.

CHAPTER 9

MEET THE FIRST LIGHT...AND DIE

Wabansi (The First Light) - was one of the great warrior leaders of the Potawatomi Nation His story is the tale of a man who seemed to know no fear. Where he walked, other men trembled. With all his great courage, in his later years, he thought not of war, but the good of his people. Like all respected elders among the ancient Algonkian speaking peoples, his thought seems to have been for the children. If, outwardly, he may have seemed ferocious, inwardly, he looked to those who would follow after him.

Wabansi, or The First Light, is an ancient Thunder Clan name. It really doesn't signify the dawn of day, but the very first, the most minute break of light in the morning sky. Like all Potawatomi names, it is a sacred name; a name brought forth from the dreams of a sacred people from time immemorial.

"Meet the First Light...and Die," may be an ill advised name for this monograph. When one speaks of his early life, it certainly seems appropriate, but the events of Wabansi's later life show him to be a man of sentiment as well as war. I would certainly liked to have met him . . . , but definitely not in a dark alley.

POTAWATOMI

The First Light (Wabansi) was a warrior chief or leader of the Potawatomi Indian Nation whose lifetime extended from about 1762 to 1847. He was born in the Old Northwest at Terre Coupe, Indiana; the son of Wahbshkum (The Dawning), and a woman called Mahjues.[1] Wabansi was the youngest of three children. His childhood name was Nahkses. His oldest brother, Mkdepoke (Black Partridge) gained notoriety at the Fort Dearborn Massacre in 1811 for repudetly saving the life of one Mrs. Helm. The story of Black Partridge is indeed interesting, but his younger brother creates even more interest. The question that surrounds the life of Wabansi is whether or not he was simply a cold blooded killer, or a patriot and hero to his own people.

To begin to understand Wabansi, one must begin to understand both the period in which The First Light lived, and something of the culture of the Potawatomi. The period in which Wabansi lived was a time of immense social and cultural upheaval for the Potawatomi. White colonization along the Ohio River was burgeoning northward into Ohio and Indiana, while further inroads where being made in the area surrounding Detroit. As if this pressure was not enough, there was almost constant savage warfare with the Creeks and Cherokees to the south and constant turmoil with Indians nations to the west - particularly the Osage and the Iowas. Wabansi grew up in the midst of all this. He was described in his youth as "being raised in the strictest pure Indian manners and customs by his parents, as his demeanor and appearance promised much to his anxious parents, and no pains were spared in watching the youth's life, examining him very closely in his dreams."[2] The young boy was noted in his youth as being of a quiet disposition; a youth who seldom spoke, though not ill-natured. As he grew into adolescence, he became a noted hunter, and he soon became a leader of war parties at a very tender age. Parents and friends tried, in desperation, to dissuade the youth from going on these war parties, but Wabansi's only answer was, "I am as much of a man as those who are going."[3] He first gained notoriety, (the year is unknown), when a group of confederated Chippewas, Ottawas, Sacs, Foxes, Kickapoos, Delawares, Shawnees, Menominess, and Potawatomies marched against the Peorias, Weas, and Piankashaws. The three tribes mentioned were doomed. It was decided in a grand council that these peoples were to be extinguished from the face of the earth. Their fires were to be put out forever. At a time and date specifiied the villages of these unfortunates were surrounded. A massacre ensued, in which Wabansi played a prominent part. All were massacred without regard to age or sex, until the few survivors begged for quarter. An old Potawatomi chief, Padegoshuk (Pile of Lead),[4] remarked years later,"...look at them (talking of the Peorias, etc.,) now they are but a handful, when once the earth appeared to small for them, but by their pride, folly, and crime, they have destroyed themselves - hence by that crisis they have called themselves our little brothers."

Potawatomi culture in the early years of Wabansi's life was very complex. Even today, there is no absolutely clear understanding of its many facets. The Potawatomi were a horticultural people, and their tribal or national domain extended along the eastern shores of Lake Michigan, down and into the southern edge of the great lake in Indiana; in Illinois, westward from the lake to the Rock River and south to Peoria. Their tribal domain extended all along the western shores of Lake Michigan also, into areas north of Green Bay, Wisconsin. The word "chief" is not properly used when speaking of these people, as they called their great men Wkamek, or leaders. Many of these Wkamek derived their authority by heredity, but could easily be displaced by others if they proved unworthy of their place in the Potawatomi scheme of life. Women Wkamek were not uncommon, and the women among the Potawatomi, had much to say over the selection of leaders.

The Potawatomi were loosely divided into Bands. Small villages were spread throughout the Old Northwest, and these villages constituted groups of families which were further subdivied into Clans. The Clan was patrilineal in nature, and naming of young people followed a system of available Clan names from the fathers forebears or ancestors. Wabansi was just such a name. It was a Thunder Clan name, much the same as his father's name before him. In the case of Wabansi, as in the case of most Potawatomi, the name took on more of a meaning then what the translation admits. The name can be variously translated (and has been) as The Early Light, A Break of Light at Dawn, A Ray of Light in the Gray, or Fog, The Eastern Light, etc., etc. An aside to this naming business is the fact that not all Potawatomi names will translate into English in what we might term, a sensible manner. If a modern day

Potawatomi speaker does not wish to divulge the meaning of a name, he or she may simply tell you that the name is untranslatable. And, it is a serious breach of etiquette to ask a Potawatomi his personal, i.e., spiritual name.

If you are told, that is fine, but to pry into what is considered none of your business - well, that is another matter.

Power! Personal power, was the crux of ancient Potawatomi ambition. Each individual person maintained a personal "guardian" or "Spirit Bundle," called Pitchkosan. Pitchkosan translates as "Watches Over Us." It is the ancient and traditional guardian or intermediary who protects and guides the individual to Kchemanito (The Great Spirit). This was the all inclusive guiding principle which guided Potawatomi thought and action. For a White man, even in this day and age, to dwelve into these mysteries can be dangerous and ill advised.

The name Potawatomi is of ancient origin, (Bode-wad-mi, or, To Make a Fire by Blowing). These people call themselves Neshnabek (People, as in Original People). As one Potawatomi has explained this to me, it separates the "Two-leggeds from the Four-Leggeds."5

Now that we have a very brief idea of the times and culture into which Wabansi was raised, it is well that we continue with his story. When questioned in the 1840's as to the meaning of his name, the then aged Wkama (singular of Wkamek) said that," When I kill an enemy he turns pale, resembling the first light of day."6 He made this comment, it seems, in a form of a twisted jest to his nephew. It was nothing but a form of Potawatomi humor. This is perhaps the keynote idea which must be kept in mind as we continue to read the adventures of the First Light. To our modern way of thinking, this would seem at best to be a morbid sense of comedy, but to the Potawatomi of old, it was a kind of high humor.

There was much that, of course, was not of a comedic nature in the life of Wabansi. His was a life of war and savagery. The first great battles of his life which are recorded are filled with a seemingly brutal and savage disposition. His want of fear bordered on desperation. He is known to have led at least three war parties against the Osages in Missouri. On the first foray against the Osages, he is said to have captured forty prisoners and killed and scalped a great number. He took for a son one of these Osage prisoners, Wazah by name, and is said to have treated him with all the tenderness he accorded his own children. Two of his known wifes were also Osage. Wabansi

Wabansi (The First Light), painted by King in 1835

Courtesy of
Anthropological Archives, Smithsonian Institution

once related the blood-curdling tale of how he did away with one of these wifes. It seems the elder wife became stubborn and contrary, at which Wabansi said to his youngest wife that she must kill the elder woman. In Wabansi's own words, he related his comment to this young wife,"If you do not kill her the first blow I will kill you."[7] The young woman did as she was bid, and Wabansi's only regret was that he was very foolish as he had given ten horses for her.

Sometime in 1794 or 1795, The First Light had his most desperate battle. He was in a war party led by his brother Black Partridge. They had gone against the Osages, who had encamped inside Fort Carondelet, in Vernon County, Missouri. This fort was owned by Auguste and Pierre Chouteau. The Osage leader was described by Wabansi as being a horned devil from the fact that he had numerous protuberences on his head. He is described as being one who bellowed like a Buffalo in keeping with his name. The affair was to be conducted at the break of day, but fog setting in, the warriors in the Potawtomi party became disheartened. Not so, Wabansi! Against the entreaties of his brother and son, he decided that he would enter the fort through a port hole. He berated the warriors in the party for being faint hearted in the following words, "I am the only brave man here. To-night I will enter the fort."[8] Black Partridge and the other warriors of the party tried to dissuade The First Light, but he was a determined man. With Black Partridge at his rear, he entered the fort with some difficulty. He found a great number of the enemy sleeping and finally came upon the horned devil described earlier. As he approached this terrible demon, he awoke, and as Wabansi struck forth with his tomahawk, he missed his blow. A second thrust was parried off with a Buffalo robe, and the horned monster bellowed in rage, and woke his fellows from their sleep. At length, Wabansi's blows began to take effect. The sleepy Osage warriors beheld their chief; his head flowing with blood. The First Light struck a brave who approached the scene and quickly took his scalp, while he swung his tomahawk in every direction to ward off the blows now being aimed at him by the furious Osage warriors. With bloody scalp in hand, he retreated towards the port hole by which he had entered. So desperate was his retreat, he left his gun behind him. The Potawatomi war party then fled to their distant homes. One scalp and a bloodied monster was the result of this sanguinary scene and quickly took his scalp, while he swung his tomahawk in every direction to ward off the blows now being aimed at him by the furious Osage warriors. With bloody scalp in hand, he retreated towards the port hole by which he had entered. So desperate was his retreat, he left his gun behind him. The Potawatomi war party then fled to their distant homes. One scalp and a bloodied monster was the result of this sanguinary attack.

In 1811, perhaps the most reknowned of all Indian leaders, Tecumseh, (One Who Passes Across Intervening Space From One Point To Another),[9] had risen to prominence in the Old Northwest. Wabansi was active in the service of this grand mentor. He claimed that he only tried to raise an army of warriors to aid the gallant Shawnee, but, in fact he probably was quite active in the various battles of that terrible war of Independence. Prior to joining Tecumseh, he was active in other theaters. In October, 1811, Wabansi succeeded in killing a boatman single-handedly on the Wabash River in Indiana.[9] This affair nearly proved fatal for the mighty Potawatomi war chief. The whole affair started as an ambush. War whoops rang out across the swift flowing Wabash River that day, and numerous volleys were fired. Upon seeing a number of the boatmen fall, Wabansi jumped into the river and attempted to swim to the raft and take the remaining boatmen captive. Upon reaching the boat, he was greeted by one of the more stallwarth fellows on board with the bitter end of a bayonet. The shiney steel blade entered his shoulder, (and here the story varies), either Wabaansi managed to pull him into the water and kill him, or else he was shot by a fellow brave on the shore. The Early Daylight was severely injured to the point of death when his son, Wazah and a friend, Megwen (The Quill) came to his aid and pulled him out of the water. It took but ten days for his wounds to heal sufficiently for him to get around, and he swore revenge against the Chemokemons (Great Knives, i.e., Americans).

A short time afterwards, he approached a stage station and attempted to steal some horses. Noise created by the horses prancing and snorting alerted the owner, and soon this stage owner was in pursuit. This was a tragic mistake. He was soon taken by surprise by the great war leader, and a large butcher knife driven through his heart. Instantly, a scalp was taken, while Wabansi cried out to his fellows, "I did not holloo when you struck me with your gun-knife,"[10] (A reference to the bayonet).

At the time of the Fort Dearborn Massacre, August 25, 1812, Wabansi is said to have been absent. Various authors have claimed that he aided his white friends after the battle, but there is no mention of his name in this connection by any of the survivors. Where he was, or what he was doing at this time is unknown. He certainly had no great affection for the White man. A best guess would be that he was absent, perhaps on some clandestine affair for Tecumseh. However, this is only speculation.

It is probable that Wabansi himself really saw "The First LIght" in the War of 1812. If he was at the battle of the Thames at Moraviantown on October 15, 1813, he certainly would have been enlightened as to the strength of the Chemokemons. With the fall of Tecumseh, and the British army under General Proctor in full retreat, the Indian allies fell into complete disarray. For the first time they saw the full power of the Chemokemons. It must have awed them beyond belief. Very few of the Indians who were involved in this affair ever after fought against the might of the fledgling nation whose numbers where like the leaves on the trees in a forest.

Wabansi seems to have disappeared from view after 1813. He reappears in historical records in 1816 when he signed a treaty of "Peace, Friendship, and Limits...on the Southwestern Parts of Lake Michigan..."11 The name on the treaty appears as "Wapunsy." Again, in 1828, he signed another treaty; a treaty which was well-oiled with whiskey. When Governor Lewis Cass told Wabansi that one of the chiefs would not sign the treaty unless he were given a bribe, Wabansi became indignant. His comment to Cass was, " An Indian who will lie, is not worthy to be called a brave. He is not fit to live. If he refuses to sanction what we agreed to in council, I'll cut his heart out." Cass later said that he had a great problem with Wabansi afterwards in preventing him from carrying out his threat. When the day of the actual treaty signing came about, an Indian debauched with whiskey stabbed The First Light. Wabansi was cared for by Agent Thomas Tipton and survived. Upon recovering, Tipton, like Cass, had a serious problem on his hands. Wabansi was going to find the Indian who stabbed him and kill him. The warrior who committed the deed was popular and a tribal feud would erupt if revenge was enacted. Tipton begged The First Light to forgive the injury. Wabansi replied, "A man that will run off like a dog with his tail down for else, he realized that the times had changed. No one knows his motives at this time. He joined, instead, with the Whites, and served with Captain Billy Caldwell and Shabi (He Has Pawed Through) as an Indian War Leader throughout the campaign.

In 1833, he signed the famous Treaty of Chicago, and here I must digress. At the Treaty of Prairie du Chien in 1829, he had been given five sections of land at the Big Woods near present day Aurora, Illinois. This had been the base village for Wabansi and his band for many years. During the Treaty of Chicago of 1833, this five sections of land was purchased from Wabansi. However, during the Treaty with the Potawatomi concluded October 26, 1832 at Camp Tippecanoe, Indiana "Wah-pon-seh and Qua-qui-to" were given five sections of land in the Prairie near Rock Village. There are three significant questions that now arise: 1. Why was Wabansi awarded land at two different areas? 2. Why did the United States government not buy back the land at Rock Village in 1833? 3. Are we, perhaps, looking at two distinct individuals with similar names?

I will here attempt to answer the third question first. Yes, we definetely have two separate and distinct individuals. We have the First Light (Wabansi), and another Band Leader named Wahpenasi (White Hawk). Thus, returning to question one, we see the possible reason for land being given at two different areas. And, to make matters worse for the United States government, the surveyed reservations given to "Wah-pon-seh and Qui-qui-to," seemed lost in the immense shuffle of reservation purchases to the present day. However, a search of War Department Records (Reserve Files) show the second reserves as being duly sold to the United States Government. Briefly, one may well ask, how does I know there were two men of similar names. First, I will mention that the two different individuals appear together in a series of documents not related to Treaties. They appear in the John Tipton Papers, in the Anderson Muster Roles from the Black Hawk War, and they appear in an enumeration of Indian Villages prepared by Pierre Menard as early as 1824. In Menard's report, Wabansi is listed as having his village on Fox river in the Big Woods, and in the same report, he says that "White Bird" is living at the Paw Paw Grove. Penasi is the Potawatomi word for bird, but when placed together with the word "Wah," AKA White, the name becomes "White Hawk." This man White Hawk was also noted as being a member of the Potawatomi exploring party of 1833, along with Wabansi - The First Light.

Menard's report, Wabansi is listed as having his village on Fox river in the Big Woods, and in the same report, he says that "White Bird" is living at the Paw Paw Grove. Penasi is the Potawatomi word for bird, but when placed together with the word "Wah," AKA White, the name becomes "White Hawk." This man White Hawk was also noted as being a member of the Potawatomi exploring party of 1833, along with Wabansi - The First Light.

In 1836 Wabansi left for his new home in Iowa. Some years after he had settled in Iowa, his remaining Osage wife left him. He returned all the way to the borders of Illinois in pursuit of her. Upon entering a Sac (Osagiwuk-People of the Inlet) lodge, and inquiring of some young men concerning his wife, the young men laughed at him. Suddenly, Wabansi stepped across the lodge, and drawing forth his tomahawk, he tapped the heads of three young men. In a most haughty manner, he addressed the chiefs and young scoffers, "Do you not know that this man who spoke to you is a great man, a brave, and a chief of the Potawatomies?" Silence reigned. An old warrior had had his say, and there was no one who would speak against him. He had won the day.

It was a lonesome man who returned to his people in western Iowa. Troubles would still beset him. Some Miamies stole a horse from him, and Wabansi waited in silence for an opportunity to right this loss. Hearing that the Agent for the Miamies was about to pay them their annuities, he took his friend Louisan and nephew Chichakose (Little Crane) with him to the Miami annuity. In a rather imperious manner, the old chief, approached the Miami chiefs and demanded payment for his horse. If not, he would take six Miami horses right in front of their eyes and dared them to stop him. This was an effrontery of no small magnitude. The Miami Agent, General John Tipton, knowing the character of the man before him, advised the Miami to pay for the horse. He further told them that Wabansi might put them to more trouble than they were aware of, and it would not do to get the old man angry. Finally, after a protracted silence, a Miami chief placed $100 dollars on the table and told Wabansi to take it. The First Light refused, and demanded that the money be placed in his hand. The Agent intervened and placed the money in Wabansi's hand, at which the old warrior replied, "That's right; now I am well pleased. If you had not paid me you would have seen hard times."[13] A few years later, the old man, while in a drinking frolic killed a respected man who had abused him. The relatives of this man buried him and said nothing more about the affair, so great was the fear and respect granted this warrior of warriors.

In 1835, this man of seventy plus winters traveled to Washington, D.C. for the first time. He had an interview with President Andrew Jackson and addressed him as Brother Brave and Warrior. Nothing of any great importance was effected by this visit. In 1837, Wabansi set his hand to another document to the Secretary of War. It was a petition in favor of having a Catholic school and missionaries from the Missouri Province attend to the Potawatomi. This document is dated 12th September, 1837.[14]

In June, 1843 Wabansi was present at a great assemblage of tribes in the Indian Territory at a place called Tallequah. The Reverend William H. Goode recorded his impressions of Wabansi, as follows: "Wau-bon-sa, a Pottawatamie Chief, said to be eighty-seven years of age; treated with great respect by those of his tribe present; complete Indian costume, with the skin of a crow split in the middle, through which his head was thrust, covering his shoulders and back, and the tail hanging down before." Goode continues his description of The First Light...: "During one of the sermons I observed in the congregation the Pottawatamie interpreter seated upon his bench with his venerable old chief, Wau-bon-sa...with several of his tribe seated near; while he, in an undertone, was, with much apparent earnestness, interpreting the sermon to them. I subsequently learned that, though his earthly pilgrimage had reached nearly ninety years, he had never before heard a Gospel sermon. He listened with seeming solemnity, and occasionally gave a nod of approval. We afterward had some conversation with him. The aged Chief expressed his conviction of the truth of what had been said. To our inquiries as to his willingness to receive schools and missions among his people, he replied that they 'wanted schools, but wished to have them established and supported by the educational fund secured to them by treaty with the Government;' thus declining any gratuitous service by the whites. In reference to missionary effort he manifested an equal spirit of independence; saying, that he would not ask them to come, but if any chose to come voluntarily and labor in his tribe he and his people would receive them kindly."[15]

One year later in 1844, we find The First Light addressing

Major Clifton Wharton in council. "Wah-baun-sey (Day Light), a very aged Chief, so old that, contrary to custom, he sat while he made the following reply: 'My friends: we are glad to see you, to have you come and encamp with us, but this land is as much yours as ours. My friends, you have had a good deal to say to others. When the Superintendent was here he told us to make improvements, as you have told us. He said look at the White people how they live, they raise plenty to eat, and never suffer. When we exchanged land for this land we made a fair exchange and we wish always to live here. I told the Superintendent I would endeavour to do like the Whites. I would take hold of the plough and do like Whites to support Wife and children. The Superintendent told us to raise corn, and we would never suffer. That is all I have got to say on this subject. Whiskey is bad, and we know it; but, what I am going to mention is as bad as Whiskey. The Ioways are as bad as Whiskey - they destroy our hogs, and I wish they could be taken out of the country. I wish they could be taken over the river - tie them round the neck and take them. We spoke to them friendly once, but wished them go over the river, but they kept saying, by and by. That is all I have got to say.'"[16]

Wabansi made a final trip to Washington in November, 1845. This visit laid the groundwork for the treaty of 1846 with the Potawatomi. The Potawatomi delegation was headed by ex-Indian agent R.S. Elliot and the Potawatomi speaker was a man named Aptegizhick (Half Day Sun). Eliiot's report of the day to day doings in Washington City puts a bit of a new "spin" on Wabansi. In reading Elliot's account,[17] we see two rather humerous individuals. Both Elliot and Wabansi spent a good deal of their time "dreaming" in their hotel rooms. Elliot dreamed of bags of gold coming forth from the government to line his pockets, while Wabansi "Dreamed" that the Potawatomi would extract everything they wanted from the authorities. This, of course, was not to be, as the Commissioners in Washington had other plans in mind.

This was to be the final journey in a long life for The First Light. On the return trip, the stagecoach overturned near Cincinnati, Ohio. The old man was suffering grieviously from the pains of old wounds and age. Some say he died before reaching home, but this is not appear to be true. Elliot published this premature death of Wabansi in his account of the journet, but Elliot had not returned with the Indian delegation. He obtained his information second hand from

Alexander Robinson in Chicago. What did MarkTwain say . . .?

There is an affidavit on file in Mills County, Iowa that states that this aged warrior became involved with the law in November, 1846 and was sued for non-payemnt of a debt of twenty-two dollars.18 An affidavit of A.L. Wolfe, a pioneer of Mills County states that, " At the time of his death the Indians wrapped the Chief's body in a blanket with peeled bark outside and placed it with his personal effects consisting of a flintlock musket, a tomahawk, beads and other ornaments in a box of thick boards split or hewn from logs. This was placed in the fork of a large oak tree about twelve or fifteen feet from the ground, the box being secured to the limbs of the tree by a chain that passed round them."

Lately uncovered by the author is a list of Potawatomi living in Iowa for the year 1847. This list contains the name Wabansi. He was to old to lead his people anymore and was settled in the village of Shati (Pelican) along Little Soldier Creek. Lastly, in May of this year (1997), I have been told by Prairie Band Potawatomi that a farmer in Mills County, Iowa has come forward and shown them the final resting place of Wabansi. Investigation continues on the site as I write.

Thus passed a light from this world. Whether this light was for good or for evil is a perplexing question for some. But, this author, feels a special kinship with Wabansi. Certainly, he was proud. Certainly, he seemed vindictive. This was the way of his people in ancient times. But, one must also look at his regrets and what he did in later life. The stories of his warrior exploits are from his own lips, but the stories must be taken for what they are - stories. Wabansi had a great sense of what might be called, sinister comedy. In telling of his life to fellow Potawatomi, he employed this satire to full sway, and now we can only really guess at what he really did during his early years. He was an adherent of the Mida religion, the ancient religion of the Potawatomi. It means, "Grand Medicine."

The First Light is now extinguished. His only son, Wapgizhek (Bright Day) died young, but the Wabansi family exists, proudly, even into this day and age. It is now night! The daylight is no more!

NOTES:

1. Originally published in the Kansas City, Missouri Enterprise of March 14 and 21st, 1857 by J(oseph) N(apolean) Bourassa, a well known metis Potawatomi leader. The story of Wabansi's life as told in this newspaper account was later reprinted in The Kansas Historical Quarterly, Summer, 1972 under the original title, "The Life of Wah-bahn-se: The Warrior Chief of the Pottawatamies."
2. Ibid note #1.
3. Ibid note #1.
4. Translation by a respected member of the tribal council of the Forest Community Potawatomi of Crandon, Wisconsin. This translation was given in an interview in May, 1989.
5. This name "Neshnabek" follows R. Landes, "The Prairie Potawatomi...," U. of Wisconsin Press, 1970 and James A. Clifton, "The Prairie People...," Regents Press, The U. of Kansas, (1977). The informant for the information regarding the distinction of "two leggeds and four leggeds," was a Lac du Flambeau Chippewa who met with the author in May, 1989.
6. Ibid note #1.
7. Ibid note #1.
8. Ibid note #1.
9. In Clifton, "The Prairie people...," and J.N. Bourassa, "The Life of Wah-bahn-se..."
10. Ibid note #1.
11. Kappler, Charles J. (ed. & comp.). Indian Treaties 1778-1883, Interland Publ. Co., New York, N.Y., (1973). Originally published as "Indian Affairs: Laws and Treaties," Vol. 2 (Treaties). Washington, D.C., 1904.
12. From Thomas L. McKenney and James Hall. "History of the Indian Tribes...," Octavo ed., Phila., 1848-49-50. Later 20th century editions titled, "The McKenney-Hall Portrait Gallery of American Indians."
13. Ibid note #1.
14. Garraghan, Gilbert J. (S.J.) The Jesuits of the Middle United States. The America Press, (1938). Rptd. Loyola University Press, 1983.
15. Goode, Rev. William H. Outposts of Zion, With Limnings of Mission Life. Cincinnati, 1864.
16. Kansas Historical Collections, Vol. XII, 1923-1925. "The Expedition of Major Clifton Wharton in 1844."
17. Elliot, Richard S. Notes Taken in Sixty Years. St. Louis, 1883.
18. The Palimpsest, Vol. XXIX, No. 12, December, 1948, Iowa City, Iowa. "Chief Waubonsie."

Additional notes...

Wabansi was involved in two stagecoach upsets, one in 1835, and again in 1845. There are conflicting stories concerning the latter accident. Some say that Wabansi died shortly after the 1845 stagecoach incident. If so, they neglect to mention his burial. If he had died near Cincinnati, his fellow travelers would surely not have carried the body back home to Iowa. The A.L. Wolfe affidavit would thus appear to state the truth. Now, in 1998, I have located Wabansi alive and living as late as 1849 in the village of Shati in Kansas.

Potawatomi names and other translations are either taken from James A. Clifton's researches among Potawatomi speakers, and have, in most cases been confirmed by this author in various interviews with Potawatomi speakers over the last two years.

     Copyright, James Dowd 1991 - Additional material added for this publication.

EPILOGUE

As I started work on the "Thunders Speak" manuscript a number of years back, I had, at my disposal a large number of monographs of various Original Peoples from almost all areas of North America. As I started to put together the various documents, it soon became apparent that the diversity of material, and the labor involved in serious research would prove to be an undertaking of an immense magnitude (not to mention confusion for myself). Thus, I have now completed what may only be part one of a series of "Thunders" documents. If my readers enjoy this initial "Thunders" work, and I sense a longing and/or need for stories of some others of those little known Original Peoples, I will easily be persuaded to continue to create more thunder sounds for my favorite people - my readers.

JPD - 1999

SELECTED BIBLIOGRAPHY

Chapter 1. All Same . . . . All Same . . . .

Annals of Iowa. 3rd Series, Vol. 16, No. 1, July, 1927.

Annual Message and Accounting Documents 1851-2, Part 3, Washington, D.C., 1851.

Armstrong, P.A. The Sauks and the Black Hawk War... Splingfield (sic), Illinois, 1887.

------------- Shabbona Memorial Association Appeal. n.p., n.d., (Ottawa, Illinois, 1897).

Barge, W. Shaubena or Shabbonee. (undated ms. in the author's possession).

Blackbird, A.J. Complete History of the Ottawa and Chippewa Indians of Michigan. Ypsilanti, Mich., 1897; rptd. Petoskey (1975).

Boies, H.L. History of De Kalb County, Illinois. Chicago, 1868; rptd. Evansville, Ind., 1973.

Campbell John. (ed. & publ.). Great Poems of the Western World. Vol II, (1990).

Clifton, James A. Chicago, September 14, 1833: The Last Great Indian Treaty in the Old Northwest. Chicago History, 1980, Vol. IX, No. 2.

--------------- On Being and Becoming Indian Biographical Studies of North American Frontiers. The Dorsey Press, Chicago, Illinois, (1989).

--------------- The Pokagons, 1683-1983: Catholic Potawatomi Indians of the St. Joseph River Valley. University Press of America, (1984).

--------------- The Potawatomi. Chelsea House, N.Y., 1987.

The Prairie People: Continuity and Change in Potawatomi Indian Culture 1665-1965. Lawrence, Kansas, Regents Press of the University of Kansas, 1977.

Correspondence and Documents of the Chicago Treaty. In Records of the Bureau of Indian Affairs. Documents Relating to the Negotiation of Ratified

and Unratified Treaties with Various Indian Tribes, 1801-1869. (T494), National Archives.
Council Bluffs Records. Jesuit Missouri Province Archives

Dowd, James P. Built Like a Bear: Which is a Descriptive Name for One of the Last Great Chiefs of the "Three Fires" in Illinois...Shabni (He Has Pawed Through). Fairfield, Wash., 1979.

-------------- Indian Paul Revere. Wild West Magazine. December, 1990.

-------------- On Becoming and Being a Neshnabe. Chicago Corral of the Westerners,1988. (awaiting publication).

-------------- The Potawatomi A Native American Legacy. St. Charles (Illinois) Historical Society, 1989.

-------------- Those Who Came Before. Fox Valley Living. December, 1989.

Drake, Benjamin. Life of Tecumseh...Cincinnati, 1841.

Gross, L.M. Past and Present of De Kalb County, Illinois. Chicago, 1906.

Hubbard, Gurdon Saltonstall. Incidents and Events in the Life of... Chicago, 1888; rptd. "Autobiography..." Chicago Lakeside Classic, 1911.

Kinzie, Mrs. J.A. Wau-bun, the "Early Day" in the North-West. New York, 1856.

Landes, Ruth. The Prairie Potawatomi: Tradition and Ritual in the Twentieth Century. Madison, The University of Wisconsin Press, 1970.

McCollough, Alameda. (ed.) The Battle of Tippecanoe: Conflict of Cultures. Tippecanoe County Historical Association, Lafayette, Indiana, 1973.

McIlvaine, C. Michigan Steamship Lines Brochure. "Shabbona" 1903.

Matson, Nehemiah. French and Indians of Illinois River. Princeton, Illinois, 1872 and 1874.

--------------- Memories of Shaubena...Chicago, 1878.

National Archives - Files B-27 and A-416.

Patterson, J.B. (Amanuensis). Life of Ma-Ka-Tai-Me-She-Kia-Kiak or

Black Hawk. Boston, 1833 and later. Titled changed to "Autobiography..." in 1888 and later editions.

Public Record Office, C.O. 42/151; 42/151. London, England.

Records - La Salle County, Illinois Courthouse.

Scanlon, C.M. Indian Creek Massacre... Milwaukee, 1915.

Temple, Wayne. Shabbona, Friend of the Whites. Outdoors in Illinois, Vol.4, No. 2, Fall-Winter, 1957; rptd. Springfield, Illinois, 1957.

Whitney, E. (ed.). The Black Hawk War. Vols. XXXV, XXXVI, XXXVII, Illinois Historical Collections, 1970-73-75.

Chapter 2. Big Foot Lake Man

Clifton, James A. The Prairie People/Continuity and Change in Potawatomi Indian Culture 1665-1965. The Regents Press of Kansas, Lawrence, (1977).

Collections of the State Historical Society of Wisconsin, Madison. Vols. II, VI, VII, VIII, XII.

Edmunds, R. David. The Potawatomi/Keepers of the Fire. University of Oklahoma Press, (1978).

Kappler, Charles J. (ed.). Indian Affairs: Laws and Treaties, Vol. 2 (Treaties). Reprint edition, Interland Publishing Co., New York, 1972.

Kinzie, Mrs. John H. Wau-Bun, the Early Day in the North-West. New York, 1856.

Matson, Nehemiah. Memories of Shaubena. Princeton Ill., 1876.

National Archives Record Group M-574, Roll 14, #98. "Emigration of Potawatomi Indians."

Patterson, J.B. (Amanuensis). Life of Ma-ka-tai-me-she-kia-kiak, or Black Hawk. Boston edition, 1834.

Portrait and Biographical Record of Walworth and Jefferson County, Wisconsin. (Chicago, 1894).

Potawatomi and Chippewa informants-names unrecorded per request of same.

165

Chapter 3. Captain Billy Caldwell: On the Reconstruction of an Abused Identity.

Self contained notes and abbreviations used in notes. See end of chapter.

Chapter 4. For He was a Bad Son

Assumption Abbey Archives - Belleau Collection.

---------- Johnson Collection.

---------- The Major James McLaughlin Papers.

---------- The Major James McLaughlin Papers; Letterbook 1878-1881.

Burdick, Usher L. (ed.). My Friend the Indian; or Three Unpublished Chapters of the Book Published Under the Title My Friend the Indian. Baltimore, 1936.

Dowd, James P. Custer Lives! Fairfield, Wash., 1982.

Graham, Col. William A. The Custer Myth/A Source Book of Custeriana..A Complete and Comprehensive Bibliography by Fred Dustin. Harrisburg, Penn., 1953.

Holley, Frances Chamberlain. Once Their Home/or, Our Legacy From the Dahkotas..., Chicago, Illinois, 1890.

McLaughlin, James. My Friend the Indian. Boston, Mass., 1910.

National Archives Record Group 98, Records of the U.S. Army Commands, Fort Totten, Letters Sent.

Newspapers

Bismarck Tribune, Sept. 9, 1881 - Nov. 25, 1874.

Fargo Daily Argus, Nov. 29, 1882.

Fargo Forum, March 4, 1946.

The Turtle Mountain Star, Jan 26, 1950.

Yankton Weekly Press and Dakotian, Nov. 16, 1882.

End newspapers...

Pfaller, Rev. Louis, O.S.B. "The Brave Bear Murder Case," in North Dakota History, Vol. 36, No. 2., Spring, 1969, Bismarck, N. Dak.

_____ (ed.). The Superior Edition of My Friend the Indian by James McLaughlin... and The Three Missing Chapters. Seattle, Wash., (1970).

Prucha, Francis Paul. A Guide to the History of Indian-White Relations in the United States. Chicago & London, (1977).

Thesis (unpublished). Milligan, E.A. The Standing Rock Sioux, 1874-1890. (U. of North Dakota).

Chapter 5. Ghost Dance Woman

Barrett, S.A. The Dream Dance of the Chippewa and Menominee Indians of Northern Wisconsin. Bulletin of the Public Museum of the City of Milwaukee, Wisconsin, Vol. 1, No. 4 (1911).

Clifton, James A. The Prairie People: Continuity and Change in Potawatomi Indian Culture 1665-1965. The Regents Press of Kansas, Lawrence, (1977).

Landes, Ruth. The Prairie Potawatomi: Tradition and Ritual in the Twentieth Century. The University of Wisconsin Press, Madison, Milwaukee and London, 1970.

Potawatomi Informants from the North Country and from the Western High Grass Plains. 1991.

Records of the Bureau of Indian Affairs - Letters Received 1881-1907. #15282.

Skinner, Alanson. A Further Note on the Origin of the Dream Dance of the Central Algonkian and Southern Siouxan Indians. American Anthropologist 25, 1923. Pages 427-8.

Skinner, Alanson. Final Observations on the Central Algonkian Dream Dance. American Anthropologist 27, 1925. Pages 340-343.

Skinner, Alanson. The Society of Dreamers. "Associations and Ceremonies of the Menominee Indians." American Museum of Natural History Anthropological Papers 13. Pages 173-182.

Chapter 6. Idaho Giant

(Elliot). History of Idaho Territory Showing its Resources and Advantages with Illustrations..., Wallace W. Elliot & Co., Publishers, San Francisco, Calif., 1884. Reprint edition of 400 bound copies, Ye Galleon Press, Fairfield, Wash., (1973).

Hodge, Frederick Webb (ed.). Handbook of American Indians North of Mexico. Washington, GPO, 1910.

Letter - Alan Virta, Head of Special Collections, Boise State University to the author dated September 19, 1991.

Letter - Terry Abraham, Head, Special Collections, University of Idaho to the author, dated August 1, 1991.

Message of the President of the United States and Accompanying Documents to the Two Houses of Congress..., Washington, GPO,1867.

Newspaper - Idaho Statesman, 1878. Original publication of Anderson's story of Bigfoot.

Newspaper - Idaho Statesman, 1919. "Gruesome Story of Tragic Death of Indian Fiend." Edited by Eva Hunt Dockery.

Newspaper - Idaho Statesman, 1919. "Bigfoot, Terror of Idaho, in Early Days of Territory Myth, Demon or Redskin?" Edited by Eva Hunt Dockery.

Newspaper - Idaho Statesman, 1919. "Bigfoot Finish Described by Man Who Saw It All." Edited by Eva Hunt Dockery.

Report on Indian Affairs by the Acting Commissioner for the Year 1867. Washington, GPO, 1868.

Schmitt, Martin F. (ed.). General George Crook His Autobiography. Norman, University of Oklahoma Press, (1960). (New edition).

Chapter 7. The Last of the Yosemites

Correspondence with UCLA and the University of California Press.

Goldman, A. American Genesis. N.Y., (1979).

Harte, Bret. The Luck of Roaring Camp and Other Sketches. Boston, 1870.
Hodge, Frederick Webb (ed.). Handbook of American Indians North of

Mexico. Washington, GPO, 1907 & 1910 (in 2 parts).

Jackson, Helen Hunt (H.H.) A Century of Dishonor... Boston, 1895. "New Edition Enlarged by the Addition of the Report of the Needs of the Mission Indians of California"

_____ Ramona A Story. Boston, (1907 Little Brown later ed.)

Kroeber, Theodora. Ishi in Two Worlds A Biography of the Last Wild Indian in North America. Berkeley & Los Angeles, 1962.

Lindquist, G.E.E. The Red Man in the United States... N.Y., (1923).

Taylor, Mrs. H.J. The Last Survivor. in the University of California Chronicle, January, 1931, Vol. XXXIII & January, 1931, Vol. XXXIV. Publication of this journal was suspended in 1933.

_____ The Last Survivor. San Francisco, Johnck & Seeger, 1932.

Van Tramp, John C. Prairie and Rocky Mountain Adventures, or, Life in the West... Colombus, Ohio, 1868.

A bibliography containing even a minimal number of journals from the gold rush days would be an undertaking well beyond the scope of this work... the author.

Chapter 8. Prophet of Disaster

Armstrong, P.A. The Sauks and the Black Hawk War... Splingfield (sic), Illinois, 1887.

Callender, Charles. "Sauk," in Handbook of North American Indians. Smithsonian Institution, Washington, 1978, Volume 15.

Clifton, James A. The Prairie People: Continuity and Change in Potawatomi Indian Culture 1665-1965. Lawrence, Kansas, Regents Press of the University of Kansas, 1977.

Cole, Cyrenus. I Am a Man...The Indian Black Hawk. State Historical Society of Iowa, Iowa City, Iowa, 1938.

Collections of the State Historical Society of Wisconsin. Madison, Wisc., various dates. Vols. I, VI, VII, VIII, X, XII, XV

Dowd, James P. Built Like a Bear: Which is a Descriptive Name of one of the Last Great Chiefs of the "Three Fires" in Illinois...Shabni (He Has Pawed Through). Fairfield, Wash, 1979.

Drake, Benjamin. The Life and Adventures of Black Hawk: With Sketches of Keokuk... Cincinnati, 1842. (7th edition).

Eby, Cecil. "That Disgraceful Affair," The Black Hawk War. New York, (1973).

Garraghan, Gilbert J., S.J. The Jesuits of the Middle United States. Chicago, Loyola University Press, 1938, (rptd. 1984), 3 volumes.

Gurkin, Miriam. Indian America: The Black Hawk War. New York, (1970).

Hagan, William T. The Sac and Fox Indians. Norman, University of Oklahoma Press, (1958).

Hodge, Frederick Webb (ed.). Handbook of American Indians North of Mexico. Washington, GPO,
1907 & 1910. Parts 1 and 2.

Kansas State Historical Society Records.

Kappler, Charles G. (ed. & comp.). Indian Affairs: Laws and Treaties. Vol. 2 (Treaties). Senate Documents, 88th Congress, 2nd Session, Doc. No. 319, Washington, USGPO, (1904), Rptd. Interland Publishing Co., New York, (1973), Vol. 2 only.

Kinzie, Mrs. John H. Wau-Bun The Early Day in the North-West. New York, 1856.

Letter of Samuel C. Stambaugh to Winfield Scott. Prairie du Chien, August 13, 1832. Photocopy in the author's private collection.

Letters received from George L. Wahquahboshkuk, Tribal Chairman of the Prairie Band of the Potawatomi Nation, particularly those of October 5, 1988 and February 24, 1992.

McCracken, Harold. George Catlin and the Old Frontier. New York, (1959).

Newspapers - Collection of newspapers in the author's collection with anecdotes and news of the Black Hawk War. The "New York Mirror," dated Saturday, July 13, 1833, the original of which is in the author's collections, contains the first known caricature of Black Hawk.

Patterson, J.B. (Amanuensis). Life of Ma-ka-tai-me-she-kia-kiak, or

Black Hawk. New York, 1834 - title changed, and with additions, "Autobiography of...," 1882.

Records Commissioner of Indian Affairs for the Year 1848. Washington, GPO, 1849.

Risteen, H.L. Black Hawk's Warpath. New York, (1950).

Sixtieth Congress, Session II, Ch. 263, Washington, GPO, 1909.

Stocking, Amer Mills. The Saukie Indians And Their Great Chiefs Black hawk and Keokuck. Rock Island, Illinois, 1926.

Stevens, Frank E. The Black Hawk War Including a Review of Black Hawk's Life. Chicago, Illinois, 1903.

Wakefield, John A. Wakefield's History of the Black Hawk War. Chicago, the Caxton Club, 1908. Ed. by Frank Everett Stevens.

Whitney, Ellen M. (ed. & comp.). The Black Hawk War 1831-1832. Collections of the Illinois State Historical Library, Springfield, 1970-73-75-78. Vols. XXXV, XXXVI, XXXVII & XXXVIII.

Chapter 8. Meet the First Light...And Die

Bourassa, J.N. In Kansas City (Missouri) Enterprise March 14 and 21, 1857. Rptd. in Kansas State Historical Quarterly, Summer, 1972.

Clifton, James A. The Kansas Potawatomi: On the Nature of a Contemporary Indian Community. Transactions of the Kansas Academy of Science 67: 1-24.

-------------- Chicago, September 14, 1833: The Last Great Indian Treaty in the Old Northwest.

-------------- The Potawatomi. Chelsea House, N.Y., 1987

-------------- The Prairie People: Continuity and Change in Potawatomi Indian Culture 1665-1965. Regents Press of the University of Kansas, 1977.

Correspondence and Documents of the Chicago Treaty. In records of the Bureau of Indian Affairs. Documents Relating to the Negotiation of Ratified and Unratified Treaties with Various Indian Tribes, 1801-1869. (T494), National Archives.

Dowd, James Patrick. Built Like a Bear" Which is a Descriptive Name for

One of the Last Great Chiefs of the "Three Fires" in Illinois...Shabni (He Has Pawed Through." Ye Galleon Press, Fairfield, Wash., 1979.

------------- The Potawatomi A Native American Legacy. St. Charles, Illinois Historical Society, 1989

------------- Those Who Came Before... Fox Valley Living Magazine, Vol 1, No. 1, November-December, 1989.

Elliot, Richard S. Notes Taken in Sixty Years. St. Louis, 1883.

The Expedition of Major Clifton Wharton 1844. In Kansas Historical Collections, Vol. XXI, 1923-1925.

Garraghan, Gilbert J. (S.J.) The Jesuits of the Middle United States. Loyola University Press, (1983). 3 Vols.

Handbook of North American Indians. Vol XV, 1978. James A. Clifton "The Potawatomi."

Hodge, Frederick Webb (ed.) Handbook of American Indians North of Mexico. Washington, GPO, 1910. (2 vols.).

Kappler, Charles G. (ed. & comp.). Indian Affairs: Laws and Treaties. Vol.2 (Treaties). Senate Documents, 58th Congress, 2nd Session, Doc. No. 319, Washington, D.C., USGPO, (1904). Rptd. Interland Publ. Co., Vol. 2 only, (1973).

Landes, Ruth. The Prairie Potawatomi: Tradition and Ritual in the Twentieth Century. Madison, The University of Wisconsin Press, 1970.

Patterson, J.B. (Amanuensis) The Life of Ma-ka-tai-me-she-kia-kiak, or Black Hawk. Boston, 1833; Boston and N.Y., 1834; Cooperstown, 1842; London, 1836; Leeuwarden, 1847. Title changed with additions, "Autobiography," Oquawka, Illinois, 1882; Chicago, 1916; Champaign, Illinois, 1955; Fairfield, Wash., 1974.

Prucha, Francis Paul. A Guide to the Military Posts of the United States 1789-1895. Madison, The State Historical Society of Wisconsin, 1964.

Swisher, J.A. Chief Waubonsie. The Palimpsest, December, 1948, Vol. XXIX, No. 12.

Whitney, Ellen (ed.) The Black Hawk War. Vols. XXXV, XXXVI, XXXVII, Illinois Historical Collections, 1970-73-75.

Abtekizhek (Half Day Sun) 61, 157

Adams, Glen iii

Adams, President John Quincy 11

Agar or Agard, Louis 81, 83, 127

Allison, Edwin H. "Fish" 82, 83, 84, 85, 93, 94

Anderson Muster Roll 154

Anderson, William T. 107, 109, 113, 114

Armstrong, Perry A. 15, 31n

Ash, Ben 79, 80, 81, 95n22

Askin, John Jr. 54

Atwater, Caleb 135, 137

Awani (Yosemite self name) 117, 118, 119, 120, 121, 130n

Battle of the Thames (Amherstburg, Moraviantown) 8, 74, 153

Battle of Tippecanoe 6

Bell, Capt. James M. 79, 93

Big Drum 150, 151, 156

Big Foot, Nampuh, Nampa, alias Starr Wilkinson. 105, 106, 107, 108, 109, 110, 111, 112, 113, 114, 115

Blackbird, Andrew J. (Mackatebenessy or Black Hawk - Odawa) 2, 16n1, 31n

Blackbird, William (Petanakwet) 2

Black Hawk War 24, 26, 198, 202, 206, 207, 228

Brant, Joseph 34, 36, 37

Butler, John 44

Caldwell, Captain Billy, (Thomas Caldwell) 8, 10, 22, 25, 28, 29, 30, 31, 32, 33, 34, 35, 36, 38, 39, 40, 41, 42, 43, 44, 45, 46, 46, 47, 49, 50, 51, 52, 53, 54, 55, 56, 57, 58, 59, 60, 61, 62, 99

Caldwell, Charles (son of Billy) 60

Caldwell, Francis 35, 44, 60

Caldwell, James 35

Caldwell, Thomas 44, 76

Caldwell, William Lt. Col. 32, 35, 33, 36, 37, 38, 44, 47, 59, 78, 79, 80, 82, 83, 84, 88

Caldwell, William Jr. 35, 40, 44, 46, 49, 49, 50, 52, 56

Cameron, Duncan 43, 48, 50, 51, 52

Cass, Governor Lewis 153

Catlin, George 134, 136

Chichakose (Little Crane) 155

Clarke, James 62

Clark, George Rogers 37

Clark, William 8, 9

Claus, William 36, 42, 47, 48, 49, 50, 51, 52, 53, 55

Clifton, Dr. James A. iii, 16n2, 23n9, 24n, 25, 45, 49, 98, 103n1, 145n21, 159n5, 160n

Cooper, Dr. John 3

Crawford, Hartley 62

Crook, Gen. George 114

Cross Village 13, 14

Custer, George Armstrong 77, 78, 142

Dawes Allotment Act x, 141

De Lormes, Joseph & family 75, 76, 80, 92, 96n32

De Smet, Fr. Pierre Jean vii, 62

Dougherty, John 61

Durnell, Reverend 21

Edwards, Ninian 8, 139

Elliot, R(ichard) S(mith) 157, 159n17

Elliot, Matthew 37, 46, 54

Elliot, Matthew Jr. 47

Fauribault, George 75, 82, 86

Flannery, George P. 80, 123

Forsyth, Robert 41

Forsyth, Thomas 40, 56, 58, 59, 60, 138

Fruit, Enoch 107, 108

Goode, Rev. William H. 156, 159n15

Goodman, Jeffrey, Dr 130

Gratiot, Col. Henry 138

Gravesett, Lt. 50, 81, 87

Hamlin, Augustin Jr. 2

Harrison, Governor William Henry 6, 8, 18, 19, 41, 42, 43, 48, 62

Heald, Captain 6

He-ha-ha-ton-ka (Night Owl, or Big Voice in the Night) 74

Holley, Mrs. F.C. 82, 95n14, 23, 24

Hubbard, Gurdon Saltonstall 9, 21, 24n, 41n3

Ironsides, George Sr. 47, 52, 54, 86, 87

Ironsides, George Jr. 54

Ish-naki-yapi (The Only One) 79

Jackson, President Andrew 156

James, Lt. Col. Reginald 48, 49, 50, 51, 52, 53

"Jesuit's Drops" 50

Johnson, Colonel R.M. 7

Johnson, Frank 107, 108,

Kack kack (Duck Hawk) 133

Kearny, Stephen Watts 97

Kiktowenene (One Who Impersonates - a speaker - Potawatomi). 58

Kinzie, John 6, 7, 19, 24n, 28, 40, 41, Known also as "Shaw-nee-aw-kee" 43,44, 49, 56, 58, 60

Kinzie, Juliette 2,14, 19, 24n1, 43, 145n12

Landes, Dr. Ruth 32n, 98, 159n5

Langis, Longie, Longie 75, 92, 93

Lebrdo, Maria. See Totuya

Lewis, Joe 106

McGill, Hugh 59

McKay, Col. William 52

McLaughlin, Major James 78, 79, 79, 80, 82. 84, 86, 87, 90, 91, 94, 95n. 96n

Mahpia Luta (Red Cloud) 92

Makataimeshekiakiak (Black Hawk) 11, 12, 134, 138, 139, 140

Makesit (Big Foot) 10, 17, 18, 19, 20, 21, 22, 23, 33

Marty, Bishop Martin 84, 86, 94

Matewaweiska (Climbing Squirrel?) Known also as "Aunt Mate," and Martha, or Martha Kack kack 15

Mato Ohitika (Brave Bear), also known as Wapepe (Smart Character) 72, 73, 74, 75, 77, 78, 79, 80, 81, 82, 83, 84, 85, 86, 87, 88, 89, 90, 91, 92, 93, 134, 135, 136, 137, 138, 139, 140, 141,142, 143, 144

Matson, Nehemiah. 3, 16n4, 32n, 43n

Matwas (Grumbler) 3

Menard, Pierre 154, 155

Mitchell, D.D. 62

Mkdepoke (Black Partridge) 151

Mkosiquah (Little Bear Woman) 15

Naught, Capt. J.S. 75, 95n7

Nebebaquah (Night Walking Woman) 3

Nibakwa (The Man Who Walks at Night) 142, 143

Norton, Major John 46

Oldham, Joe 115

Padegoshuck (Pile of Lead), Potogoees vii, 148

Palmer, Edmund 77, 78, 79, 89

Patterson, J.B. iii, 32n, 43n

Peckwani, Peckwano (Smoke) 3, 12

Pfaller, Rev. Louis 72, 74

Pkuknoquah (Bear Clan Woman) 3,5, 15

Proctor, Colonel Henry, later Brigadier General 7, 48, 78, 97

Prophet (See Wabokishiek)

Rain in the Face 77, 118

Reynolds, Lonesome Charley 77

River Raisin 43

Robinson, Alexander, also know as Chechebinquay (The Squint Eye). 10, 40, 56, 90, 158

Russel, Captain J.B.F. 14

Sauganash, Sakonosh (Englishman - Actual translation is "He Sails Far and Wide") See Caldwell, Captain Billy

Sayer, Capt. Edward 53

Sebequah (River Woman) 15

Shabni (He Has Pawed Through), Shaahb-knee, Chabona, Shabbona, Shabbonah, Shabehnay, Shahbehney, Shaubena, Shabenee, Shobbonier, Chevalier, Chamblee, Chambli, Chambly, Shabenal, Shaubeanee 2, 3, 4, 6, 8, 9, 10, 11, 12, 13, 14, 15, 26, 27, 28, 29, 54, 58

Shannon, Oliver 84, 85, 86

Shau-nosh-ka (First Lightning From the South). See Wahquahboshkuk, George L.

Shawnee King, see Tenskatawa

Shati (Pelican) 158

Shelby, George 7

Shemargar, Shamagar (Soldier) 10, 11

Shobbomnier, Francis Shobbonier, Chevalier, confused with Shabni name 6

Sitting Bull (Tatanka Iyotanka), Hunkpapa Lakota of Little Big Horn fame. 82, 83, 93, 142, 143

Slocum, Lt. Herbert J. 79

Stephens, E. 100, 101, 155

Stillman, Isaiah 12, 140

Stillman's Run, battle of 140

Sunk-sa-pa (Black Horse) 74

Tecumseh 3, 6, 8, 32, 42, 43, 70, 71, 74, 86

Tenskatawa (the Shawnee Prophet and brother of Tecumseh) 49, 50, 152

Tipton, John (Papers) 229

Tipton, John 154

Tipton, Thomas 153

Topnebi (He Sits Quietly) 3

Totuya (Foaming Water), alias Maria Lebrado 117, 118, 120, 121, 123, 124, 125, 126, 127, 128, 129

Van etten, Thomas. 78, 79, 142

Van Slyke, James 21, 23

Wabansi (The First Light), Nahkses 146, 147, 148,149, 150, 151, 152, 153, 154, 155, 156, 157, 158. 160n

Wabenasi (White Hawk) 154,155

Wabokishiek, Wa-be-ka-shick (White Cloud) 11, 12,131, 132, 134, 135, 136, 137, 139

Wabzhick (White Cloud-Potawatomi) 133

Wahacankaduta (Red Shield) 74, 78, 81, 90, 91, 94

Wakwaboshkuk (Fish in Roiled Water) 131, 132, 133, 140, 141,142, 143

Wahquahboshkuk, George L. 131, 132, 133, 141, 143, 145n1

Wahquahboshkuk, Levi. 143

Wananikwe, Wananiquah (Strange Woman) 97, 98, 99, 101, 102

Waunoshick 135

Wayne, General Anthony 2, 8

Waywash (Bad Girl) 15

Wharton, Major Clifton. 157

Wheeler, John M. 107, 109, 112, 113, 114, 115

Willard, Rev. George L. 88, 89, 137

Wilson, Captain John 45, 47, 48, 53, 55

Wilson, James Grant 3

Wkama (sing.); Wkamek (plural), leader, leaders 10, 22, 28, 29, 61, 63, 142, 148, 149, 150

Wolcott, Alexander 28, 58

Yates, Capt. George W. 77

Zebequah, Sebequah (River Woman) 3, 29

www.ingramcontent.com/pod-product-compliance
Lightning Source LLC
Chambersburg PA
CBHW071202160426
43196CB00011B/2169